CW00766105

MODELLING
The Southern Region
1948 TO THE PRESENT

Excellent Southern Region electric stock such as this 4COR is a feature of Paul Hopkins' Retford in 3mm scale.

MODELLING
The Southern Region
1948 TO THE PRESENT

CHRIS FORD

THE CROWOOD PRESS

First published in 2017 by
The Crowood Press Ltd
Ramsbury, Marlborough
Wiltshire SN8 2HR

www.crowood.com

© Chris Ford 2017

All rights reserved. No part of this publication may be reproduced or transmitted in any
form or by any means, electronic or mechanical, including photocopy, recording, or any
information storage and retrieval system, without permission in writing from the publishers.

British Library Cataloguing-in-Publication Data
A catalogue record for this book is available from the British Library.

ISBN 978 1 78500 300 4

Dedication
For Karen.

Acknowledgements
The author would like to extend his grateful thanks to the following for their kind
assistance: Simon Hargraves, Nigel Hill, John Wright, the Bluebell Railway, the East Kent
Railway, the Lavender Line and the Swanage Railway.

Typeset by Jean Cussons Typesetting, Diss, Norfolk
Printed and bound in India by Replika Press Pvt Ltd

CONTENTS

CHAPTER ONE

INTRODUCTION

WHAT IS THE SOUTHERN REGION?

The Southern Region: what is it, and what did it do? More to the point, and because this is a book primarily about modelling, what precisely does the Southern Region have to offer as a subject for the railway modeller? It is very unlikely that these questions will be answered in anything near a complete way, but what is hoped is that a thought process will be opened up, which might get the reader a little closer to these answers.

A book is usually written with a particular reader in mind. In this case it is assumed that the imagined reader is probably not a modelling expert, maybe not even yet a modeller, but possibly someone who is in that first flush of enthusiasm, or maybe an existing railway modeller who has tried a few generic pieces of model work and is looking to find a more specialized beginning point, and needs to be led gently through the door to a particular modelling subject. And it is likely that in some ways this probably covers 99 per cent of all railway modellers at least once in their lifetimes.

The classic Southern Region scene at Plumpton in 2015, with a spread of history: nineteenth-century LBSCR signal box, BR(S) hand-operated gates and late 1990s 'Southern' 377-class electric unit.

The way it was for the Southern modeller: Wrenn R1, Hornby E2 and Hornby Dublo West Country 4-6-0.

We will all take a casual look over the fence from time to time at an unknown area of railway prototype, and wonder how that area works and how to approach it by the most logical route. In that way the Southern Region is like any other: it has its fans, its haters, its experts, and people who look over that fence and think to themselves, 'I wonder what's going on over there, and could I do that?'

This book hopes to give a few answers to the first part of the question, and gives a resounding 'Yes, you can' to the second part. Modelling the Southern Region is no more difficult than anything else, and in recent years has become much more straightforward to do (at least in 4mm scale), due in part to commercial manufacturers waking up to the idea that it's not too specialist and is actually very popular. There are still gaps in the availability of some prototypes, particularly mid-sized 'ready-to-run' (RTR) locomotives and coaching stock, but these are gradually being resolved, and if you are that modeller looking over the fence, then there is enough to get you started, and plenty to keep you

going for quite a while before you need to worry about those gaps.

THE MODELLING POPULARITY SHIFT

There was a time when the Southern, either in its Railway or Region form, was a rather dark art. In the popular scale of 4mm (OO gauge) there was very little available from any of the commercial manufacturers – in fact, going back twenty-five years or more, all the prospective modeller really had on offer was the following: an ex-South East and Chatham Railway Class R1 from Wrenn, a Hornby Dublo West Country class, an ex-London Brighton and South Coast Railway Class E2, and a Southern Railway Lord Nelson Class from Hornby, of which only the West Country was anything close to a dimensionally accurate model. In addition there were a couple of items from Tri-ang dating from the 1960s in OO and TT scales, which were no match for the crisper productions of the mainly Chinese moulding techniques of the late 1970s and beyond.

The only ways to build a Southern Region locomotive stud were to use white-metal kits or to scratch-build, and these techniques are not for everyone, especially the less confident novice. In N gauge the situation was an almost non-existent range of items, and in the larger O gauge the idea is, and always has been, that you will build most of your rolling stock from kits anyway. Compare all this to the seemingly endless stream of models for the Western Region and Midland Region modeller, and it's no wonder that the luckless Southern fan was definitely seen as the poor relation.

All this changed in the late 1980s with a model from the relatively new manufacturing name of Dapol. The ex-London, Brighton and South Coast Railway (LBSCR) Terrier in OO scale was an instant success, and was quickly issued in a range of the prototype liveries that the locomotive had carried, including British Railways, Southern, and the Marsh umber brown of its original building company, the London, Brighton and South Coast Railway. From this point on the Southern Region modeller received a definite boost in interest, with new, RTR models being released with every manufacturer's annual announcements.

The situation today is that commercially available models of the Southern Railway and Southern Region have almost overtaken those of the other main three regions in numbers and popularity, with most of the important mainline passenger locomotives available ready to run, and also selected examples of the later mainline coaching stock. There are gaps, of course, and many of these gaps can be plugged by returning to our old friend the kit and a little gentle scratch-building, but most of the hard work is already done.

The other surprising change is the rise in popularity of the Southern Region Electric Multiple Unit (EMU), once very much scorned by the Southern Region steam locomotive fans, but which are now equal in both prototype study and in sales of the model versions, which are fast coming on stream in RTR form.

So at least in 4mm scale (OO) the future seems very bright, and it would appear that if your interest is in the Southern Railway/Region, then you will have picked a very good time to start. Even if that interest leans towards an even smaller scale, then in N gauge there is enough to at least get you started, with an ex-London and South Western Railway Class M7, Southern Railway N classes from Graham Farish, and the Brighton A1X Class 'Terrier' from Dapol following on from its success with the 4mm-scale version.

With all these RTR items available, the questions are: where is the actual 'hands on' modelling, and what is there to model? The following chapters of this book make a few suggestions as to the first question, with a number of easy entry projects aimed squarely at the new and novice modeller, one who wants to be a little more ambitious and thoughtful. Along the way suggestions will be given as to how these particular project items could be fitted into a layout, that layout's geographical setting, and in some instances how adaptations can be made to shift that setting with the minimum of fuss.

Of course historically the Southern Region is a very large subject, and geographically quite a large and diverse area, so specifics must be dealt with in terms of what and where. Therefore although the whole region will be discussed, the modelling sections will revolve largely around the central section – the old LBSCR area – because this enables the greatest number of commercial items to be used. Also mindful of the fact that most modellers will be saddled with that eternal modeller's problem, a lack of physical domestic space available for a layout, the suggestions will generally be aimed at smaller ventures, as it is always easier to make a small project plan bigger, but rarely as easy to make a big project plan smaller.

MODELLING THE SOUTHERN POST-1948 'REGION'

The title of this book uses the word 'Region'. This is very deliberate and reflects the fact that the majority of modellers will be looking at one of the time

BR 4-6-0 (4MT) Class 4 at Sheffield Park. Built from 1951, the last was withdrawn in 1968. They were designed for mixed traffic use on secondary routes, where the Class 5 would be too heavy. They used the same running gear as the standard 2-6-4 tank engine, with the leading bogie from the Standard Class 5. Design work was done at Brighton, but the locomotive was built at Swindon.

periods post-nationalization, and not the slightly more specialist Southern 'Railway' in its 1923–48 private company form, or one of the Southern Railway's pre-group (that is, pre-1923) constituent companies. These would require a far more detailed approach than is allowed for here, and as is explained above, the majority of the commercial items available suit this post-nationalization period very well – although it has to be said that many have their design roots in the earlier periods, so it would take only a small further step to backdate some of the projects within the book as a jumping-off point,

for example to the LBSCR in 1920 if that is your interest. Some suggestions will be made along the way, if this is appropriate – which leads us neatly to the first of the tips that will be scattered randomly throughout the book.

THE HISTORICAL SHAPE OF THE SOUTHERN REGION

What will become apparent as this book unfolds is that the Southern Region, which is generally abbreviated to BR(S) – or, come to that, any nationalized

TIP: DECIDE WHAT YOU WANT TO ACHIEVE

Spend some time deciding what you want to achieve in terms of scale, period and size of the overall project before you buy too much or start work on a layout. The sub-tip is, don't 'over-reach' at this stage. A small, fully worked out layout plan that can be finished in a reasonable time is better than a grandiose, epic, room-filling idea that will never have a chance of getting done. The key point is often to work out as part of the scheme how much time realistically you have available, as this is probably more important than the layout plan itself. It doesn't matter how many or how large a plan you dream up in your head during your working or commuting hours: if you have only twenty minutes of spare time a day outside work and family commitments, then a big layout simply won't get done.

It is a far better policy to start small, pace yourself, and build something that can be regarded as finished within a reasonable amount of time. A project that is likely to take longer than a year to get basically finished will quickly lose impetus, and will become a millstone and not a pleasure.

Southern Region starting signals on a steel post with lattice doll posts at Sheffield Park.

region really – rarely does quite what you expect it to. Possibly due to the way that model manufacturers present their goods, or because of the way that certain key books and magazines have illustrated things, we all have a preconceived and even a slightly rosy view of what happened to the railways after World War II. Much of the time this view is highly inaccurate, and while it would be impossible for this book to document and detail every part of it, it will encourage the reader and modeller to look a little more closely, and not blindly accept what is often presented as non-movable historical fact. And historical is precisely what it is, making us in a small way social historians, because the railway – any railway – is tied up with the people it carried and the time it existed, and the two cannot be separated.

The start of the given period (1948–94) is some seventy years ago, a time of extreme material shortages, rationing – which, incidentally, didn't completely end until some ten years after World War II – and a drop in available man-power. In complete opposition to that was the public feeling that this was a brave new world where the British people, government and industry were all in high spirits and generally very positive: after all, we had won the war and now anything was possible. These two opposing realities threw up some interesting results on the railways, some of which look completely nonsensical in hindsight. However, we cannot change that, and the task of the railway student and modeller is to look back at the available information and to replicate the feel of the ages, of which there are, in rough terms, two definite eras.

FIRST OR SECOND SOUTHERN REGION PERIOD?

Visually speaking there are roughly two periods of the Southern Region: the first runs from the end of World War II to 1968, and the second from 1968 to 1994. The first looks, sounds and smells much like the railway did before the war, while the second is much different – a switch is flicked, you could say literally – as the Southern Region shakes off the past and at least partly completes the plan that was dreamed of by the previous company in the 1930s: the use of electricity to power trains throughout the region.

Of course there is much cross-over between the two periods, but it is fairly safe to say that the modeller of the Southern Region will fall on one side of the line or the other: pre-1968 with steam, or post-1968 without. It really is that simple, and both mindsets will have their fans and their detractors. What is noticeable is that modellers who favour both are rare indeed. The limited Southern Region diesel traction will sit nicely in the middle and is acceptable to either, but only a few will mix steam and third rail electric motive power on the same layout.

THE LOCOMOTIVE AND NOT THE TRAIN

Freight on the Southern is another badly presented and inaccurately modelled area. True, there was slightly less of it on the Southern Region, but the problem for the modeller is that two factors play against the study of what there was of it: first, a very large proportion of it was moved at night, and while modern digital cameras will cope well with low light situations, film stock doesn't. And of course pre-1994 we are dealing with film only.

The other problem is that the further back in time you travel, the greater the expense factor. The people who were photographing railways generally favoured passenger trains and locomotives, and few wanted to point their cameras towards any filthy dirty, uninteresting freight traffic, especially when the film-stock media that they were using was relatively expensive to buy and process. The result is that where freight trains were photographed, the locomotive at the head of the train is the star with the classic nose-on, three-quarter view to the fore. What's behind the locomotive is not considered highly, and the poor old brake van at the rear is a dot in the unfocused distance.

To a lesser degree the same problems apply to hauled coaching stock. The Southern Railway (and Region) was incredibly thrifty and had a penchant for recycling stock with alarming enthusiasm. Old bodies were re-mounted and converted into pull-push units, and old underframes had new bodies mounted on them or new electric units built on to them. This meant that, to the casual observer, visually it didn't change that much, especially with regard to the common suburban stock, with many pre-grouping (pre-1924) company designs lasting until the end of steam.

The net result of this is that the photographer pointed his viewfinder at the new and exciting items, and not the ordinary. Bizarrely, and with not a small amount of irony, the Southern Railway's Q1 Class 0-6-0 goods engine, which was designed to be as stripped down and plain as possible, had everybody taking photographs of it simply because it was new and decidedly quirky in its outward austerity-driven appearance.

So what follows is a little of everything: some history to fire your desire to know more, some very basic planning ideas, some kit building, some architecture study, and the subsequent construct-ing of some of these – and probably less of the glamour than most modelling books. This is less express train and more 'down in the dirt', to find out what made the Southern Region unique – and as a modeller, how you can make your layout scream 'Southern Region' by using as many of the commercial items that are available in model shops with a little ingenuity.

There are plenty enough of these available now, especially in 4mm scale, and while they are in the main very good quality, the question that hangs over the novice is how to use them in an effective way without over-crowding them or placing them inaccurately. There is a certain amount of 'art' in this, but it is not impossible for the enthusiastic beginner, armed with a few quality period-photo album-type books from which to work, to arrange these items in such a manner that will imply more experience.

The key to most of this lies in pure observation, and to a certain extent patience, both allied to a few artistic rules of visual balance. In many – and possibly most – cases, total prototype accuracy is not the end to aspire to: more often it is a question of taking particular key elements and combining them

Hastings colour light starter signal having just turned to danger after releasing the Cannon Street-bound Class 375 (see the opposite view of the semaphore signals at the other end of the platform in the signal section later in the book). Note the trap siding behind the speed limit sign.

Oliver Bulleid's ugly duckling: the Q1.

in a natural fashion. It is often true that many layouts that depict a location down to the last degree of accuracy lack feel and warmth, whereas those that maybe compress the site slightly, but keep the key elements mentioned above, gain more compliments from third-party viewers and give the modeller more pleasure.

That is not to say that the highly super-accurate layout build is wrong, only that holding this up as the ultimate goal can confuse and deter the novice, where a slightly more artistic approach that produces a less stunningly accurate but well produced layout is more likely to get finished. As mentioned earlier, this 'getting it finished' is a far more admirable goal that getting it perfect. Better to run the race with an old pair of trainers and reach the finishing line, than continually put off running at all for want of the perfect, brand new expensive pair.

GET OUTSIDE AND OBSERVE THE RAILWAY

The Southern Region modeller is lucky in that there are half-a-dozen well run preserved lines in the area. It is recommended that you visit these, and take in as much of the surroundings and atmosphere as you can. Even so, preserved lines are, by their very nature, only shadows of the real thing. On the whole they exist to shuttle tourists up and down in rolling stock of fixed formations, and cannot replicate the true historical steam-age railway: there are few or no connecting trains, no attached and detached coaches to attend to, no porters pushing barrows up and down platforms, and no long, dirty, slow-moving freight trains clanking through the station in a quiet period to change the mood. This is not meant to denigrate them in any way, but only to point out to the modeller that

Preserved EPB (electro-pneumatic brake) unit on the East Kent Railway.

although there is much to be taken away from a visit, he should also understand that this is far from the whole story.

The modeller of the second electrified post-1968 Southern Region period is even less lucky. There are, as yet, no preserved lines in the region that are run using electric power – safety regulations keep this strictly in the hands of the mainline companies. There are, however, several lines operating 'Thumpers' – the colloquial all-encompassing name for the Southern Region's diesel-electric multiple units (DEMU). Once again it is recommended that if you are modelling this second post-1968 period, a view and a ride on some of these preserved DEMUs is all but compulsory to gain the feel of how they sound and operate. There are, incidentally, plenty of

modern DEMUs running on the mainline system in the south, but they certainly don't have the audible appeal of the Thumpers, the engine noise of which can be heard for miles.

ATMOSPHERE

The key, then, isn't so much about what you buy, how much you spend, or exactly what you do. What is important is to gain the atmosphere of the workings of the rich and varied Southern Region, from the rapidity and the lack of funds of the Kentish lines, to the slower pace of the ends of the North Cornwall steam branches.

The aim of this book is to get you modelling (note *modelling* and not just buying: purchasing a ready-to-run model in a box is not modelling, only acquisition). The text is broken up into chapters, but these are not meant to be read or followed in order: rather, they should be selected according to your interest and the task that you wish to carry out. The emphasis is very much on the hands-on, practical experience, for while it is quite possible to buy a Southern Region layout off the shelf of the model shop or internet (and many do), the pleasure in most cases is gained by making something yourself, either from a kit or by scratch-building, or at the very least, by adding a little real coal into a locomotive bunker or tender.

The chapters are structured with some easy-build projects at the start, and progress to assemblies of track and line-side equipment that are still not too complex. If modelling in 4mm scale it is assumed that many of the locomotives and some coaching stock will be purchased ready to run, so the accent is on attempting to improve these by adding a couple of things to each to gain realism and possibly give them a human touch. To build a complete demonstration layout that covered absolutely everything would be impossible, as the subject is too wide. So the overriding assumption is that most modellers will be looking at a pre-1968 steam-age branch or secondary line, and most of the practical projects will therefore be focused in that direction, although much of the later period and the third rail system will also be discussed.

'Thumper' Class 207 DMU at Uckfield shortly to depart for Oxted, probably in its last livery of Network SouthEast. A few Thumpers made it into Connex yellow before all the Oxted line slam-door stock was consigned to the scrapheap, to be replaced by new Class 171 DMUs.

CHAPTER TWO

WHAT TO MODEL

FAILING TO PLAN IS PLANNING TO FAIL

So you have decided on the Southern Region as a subject, and let us assume that you have chosen the logical 4mm scale (OO). Further to that, let us also assume that you have a few pieces of 4mm-scale equipment that may or may not be suitable. This is good: even if they don't fit the overall brief, they can be used in the planning stages as props.

So where do you start? Well, ideally you need to make a few paper plans, and these could include several different aspects such as domestic space, cash considerations, your own ability and, as already mentioned, the often forgotten aspect of how much spare time you have. However, there is still one overriding question: what do you want the model to be, and what do you want it to do? Here are a few possibilities:

- A grand, epic mainline that fills the loft/garage/spare room
- An L-shaped through-station secondary line along two or three room walls
- A large urban terminus
- A small exhibition layout
- A compact country terminus
- A motive power depot

Southern Region preservation at its finest: the Swanage Branch just north of Corfe.

Any one of the above is perfectly feasible. The first two will take a lot of time and will cost a considerable amount. The last two suggest something that could be finished within a reasonable time scale, with the country terminus being the most economic. It would also be possible to exhibit any of these, although this needs careful thought, and other non-modelling factors need to be allowed for, such as transport, weight, portability and public operation issues.

This particular question is deliberately introduced very early as it can have quite a profound effect on how a layout is designed and built, so it needs to be considered right from the start. A home layout needs to be front operated, and will probably not need too much in the way of lighting, display boards or portable power units – but an exhibition layout most probably will, and these need to be factored in to the design and thought process.

BEING SENSIBLE

Many years ago not only was railway modelling a rich man's pursuit, it was also a very mainline affair.

Even the clockwork gauge O tinplate toys of the time had mainline pretentions, despite being short, dumpy 0-4-0s. As the hobby became cheaper and the scale smaller, the view was put about that the way to get into the hobby was to start with a branch-line terminus, and work this into a mainline layout as funds allowed. The upshot of this idea was that branch lines became not only the start point, but contrary to the original idea, the finish as well – and now it is difficult to shake off this concept and many see it as the only way to do things.

However, the primary idea is a sound one, because even if you have dreams of a room-filling mainline railway, starting with a smaller branch terminus does two things: first, it means you can learn the modelling techniques before spending too much on large infrastructure; and second, it enables you to build your collection of rolling stock gradually without it looking lonely and inadequate. After all, there is no point having a double garage full of a model of Waterloo station if you have only one locomotive and one coach. A small branch terminus will ease you in gently, and can always be broken up for parts or sold on as the bigger layout emerges.

Brighton 'Lovers' Walk' depot in the late 1970s with a Class 33 diesel and two Class 73 electro-diesels in view, not to mention a brace of CIG and BIG EMU stock on the stabling lines.

The same applies to the motive power depot (MPD) idea. Some of these were quite compact, and are ideal if you have limited domestic real estate to play in. An MPD will allow you to build up locomotive power and still have a logical place to display and run it, and of course there is also ample excuse to run freight wagons in and out for works supplies and fuel. Even the occasional piece of carriage stock will not look out of place.

A PROTOTYPE BASE

Another mantra is 'base your model on the prototype and not on other people's models': this is sound advice, and with the MPD idea, it is fairly easy to find real situations to copy. Outside the main Southern Railway works of Ashford, Eastleigh and Brighton there were many minor works and running sheds, from the large, such as Guildford, to the tiny, such as the still extant shed at Swanage, which were open up to the end of steam. However, before that the Southern Railway had miles of lines

for cleaning and storing both diesel and electric multiple units, and post-1968 it was quite logical to combine these with the locomotive sheds, such as in the view of Brighton in the photograph. Of course, post-1968 the requirement for sheds and workshops dropped dramatically, since the maintenance levels demanded by diesels and electrics were far less than those of steam locomotives, so although they may have still existed, they were far fewer in number.

Thus a perfect start point for the steam-age modeller would be a small running shed where locomotives are cleaned and kept overnight, with some sort of physical boundary such as a high retaining wall to give an excuse for a cramped site. The post-1968 modeller need only look at the photo to get some ideas on how to arrange a more modern complex.

The small branch-line terminus is more of a problem, especially if you want to keep to the prototype. Unlike the Western Region, which had plenty of neat branch termini still operating into

Class 73 electro-diesel awaiting its next turn on the west side of Brighton station.

Hayling Island station site. The goods shed, still recognizable as such, is now a small theatre. The passenger platform sat roughly where the cyclists are, the line disappearing north towards Langstone Bridge and Havant behind the new gate.

British Railways days, the Southern Railway had lost most of its likely candidates before World War II. Furthermore, while the Western Region stations were still often driven by steady, if declining, goods traffic – passengers having long since deserted them for the bus service (often the GWR's own) – the Southern Region's remaining single-track branches existed for one thing only: holidaymakers.

This meant that many of what you would expect to be nice, compact branch termini were anything of the sort. Seaton in Devon is often cited as a perfect plan, but usually in its original 'as built' state, and not as it appeared after the Southern Railway had levelled the site, enlarged the whole thing and put up a classic Southern concrete station building. This

story is repeated all along the south coast, with short branches not being designed for a steady, modest flow of general traffic, but for fast turna-round, long trains that needed to load or disgorge large numbers of holidaying people very quickly.

ARTISTIC LICENCE

What the modeller has to do, as indicated in the introduction, is use a little artistic licence, commonly known as 'freelancing'. There is nothing derogatory about this: many modellers who preach about the perfection of prototype modelling rarely produce anything that has not been compressed in some way, or has the correct rolling stock augmented with 'other items'. For instance, pretty branch termini such as Hayling Island or Lyme Regis operated with only one type of locomotive power through much of their lives – but this doesn't mean that you shouldn't model something based on them and vary the model motive power. A logical way to approach this, especially for the beginner, is to take elements of two or three different but similar sites, and combine them to create something that gives the best and widest range of options.

THE LOOK OF THE SOUTHERN

Another worthwhile piece of advice is, 'you should be able to identify the place and area without any trains in view'. This again is mostly true, and what it actually means with regard to our particular subject is that it should be possible for the viewer to recognize that he or she is looking at a Southern Railway/ Region layout before the Q1 Class and its goods train appear. The recognition should be possible by using only a small amount of information. This is so fundamental to the modelling that it's worth repeating: *the recognition should be possible by using only a small amount of information.*

If you glance back at the photo of Plumpton crossing at the beginning of the Introduction, this is readily apparent. In your mind's eye remove the Class 377 electric unit from the scene and look at what is left. In this case three items set the place:

A quick way to get a Southern Region flavour is to focus on the green signage. The architectural styles varied greatly across the system, but the green signs were a consistent thread. Adding this seemingly small detail will really give a sense of place.

Geographical details help to set the scene. Even without the giveaway of the third rail and the LBSCR box, the chalk in the background places the railway firmly in the South Downs.

the concrete, the LBSCR box, and the third rail. On their own (the box excepting) these do not work: concrete is ubiquitous and the third rail is used in other locations in the UK, but in combination the sense of place jumps out at the viewer. Therefore what we need to do on a model is to establish this type of combination to create a typical, but not contrived scene that tells the viewer where the layout is set. In doing this the appearance of a Southern Region train is enhanced ten-fold, as it looks right and the overall scene is complete.

This does not mean that you have to include every Southern Region modelling item in your layout – in fact this is best avoided. What you *do* need to do is decide where you want the layout set, and which items will best set the scene in the most natural way,

and which tell the viewer that this scene is typical of the prototype, even if the whole thing is basically freelance. Here are a few examples:

- Green paint on signs and woodwork
- Concrete platforms, footbridges and fencing
- Concrete 'quadrant'-style lamp-posts
- Third rail pick-up
- Constituent company – LBSCR, SER, LSWR – signal boxes
- Southern Railway rail-built signal posts

The other pre-train angle is to use geology. Although the majority of the Region's underpinning is made up of other formations, chalk will set the scene just as quickly as any of the above list. This is due more

TIP: USE LOCAL DETAILS TO SET THE SCENE

Look at the general area in which you wish to set your model, and take note of factors such as geology, building materials and styles, and other local details. Even if you live out of the Southern area, photo books and internet study such as Google Earth can give you all you need without having to leave your house.

to what people would expect to see, rather than the reality. To some extent this type of approach flies in the face of any requirement to get it 'right', but used as another clue to the sense of place, this slight twisting of geological fact works wonders and can be used very effectively on a small layout; thus a small cutting – for instance possibly edging a goods yard – will indicate a southern downland setting. Chalk is not easy to replicate, but even a small area will gain the recognition factor.

34070 MANSTON was the last locomotive to be built by the Southern Railway before nationalization in 1948, here seen preserved at Swanage. The SR West Country and Battle of Britain classes (collectively known as Light Pacifics) were designed to be lighter in weight than their sister locomotives the Merchant Navy Class, and were used on a wide variety of routes as mixed traffic power, being equally adept at hauling passenger and freight trains; they were also used on all types of service, frequently far below their capabilities. A total of 110 locomotives was constructed between 1945 and 1950, named after West Country resorts or subjects associated with the Battle of Britain.

APPLYING THE SENSE OF PLACE TO ROLLING STOCK

The late Bob Barlow, the ex-editor of *Model Railway Journal*, is often quoted as saying 'It is the art of the typical which convinces'. This gem of sage thought should be pinned on the wall of every modelling room. What Bob Barlow meant, was that in order to make a scene on a layout believable it should demonstrate and reflect the most likely of background and rolling stock and avoid the unusual, special or quirky elements. We all love to run favourite stock – and that is all well and good, but if we, in this case, want to model the Southern Region at a particular period of time, then the models we buy or build should reflect what the Southern typically looked like and not how we imagine it looked like. This point has been touched upon earlier, the non-acceptance of what the model manufacturers push at us; instead, try to look closely at what really happened, and try to get the look and feel of it.

'Try' is used deliberately. We do not, as a rule, have acres of space or the time to replicate everything exactly, especially when it comes to linear ground measurements. What we can do is 'try' to gain the feel of what went on with the background as detailed above, and particularly with the rolling stock. Before you buy a ready-to-run model or a kit, ask yourself why you are doing this, and attempt a little research. For example, you may be modelling the Central area of the Southern and wish to purchase a T9 Class 4-4-0 locomotive. These were based at Battersea for a while and worked many ex-LBSCR lines, but it is only a small window early in nationalization. After that the remains of the class were pushed westwards on to ex-LSWR metals. So having a T9 is possible, but far from typical.

There is a problem in that the more you find out,

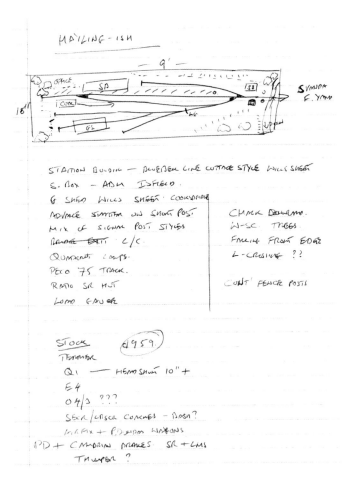

Emptying your ideas on to paper as a 'back of an envelope' sketch with stock ideas and design thoughts saves much time in the long run.

the harder things get, and as you study the histories of specific locomotives and stock, where they ran and what sort of trains they might have hauled, the fussier you will become. If you want to get the 'feel' right, then this 'art of the typical' should be the question you ask over and over again. If this is used as your mantra then the result will be far more satisfying and realistic than if you just follow the modelling crowd and design your layout out of the ready-to-run manufacturers' catalogues. Note that 'accurate' was not used: there is a difference. If 'accurate' is your aim, then all well and good, but a far more achievable goal is 'typical'. Find that typical and overwhelmingly Southern feel, and the magic will appear. Make just 'accurate' your goal and you may get it perfect, but you will miss the 'feel' by a country mile.

The theory of this is easy enough to deal with, and of course the same arguments could be levelled at any railway model in any scale from anywhere in the world. The attitude of 'typical' over 'highly accurate' is a well worn path. It has to be said, though, that some layouts have it, and some don't, and a lot of the time it is this 'typical' that tips the balance. How, then, do you go about it in real terms? The best way is to choose your subject – say, a branch terminus – and gather as much visual information as possible. It doesn't have to be all concerning the same line: it could be a combination of lines, as outlined above. Then sketch out a plan. This could take the form of track diagrams and signal positions, but also a list of items that may be applicable. This could take the form of a rough list with accompanying sketches on a sheet of A4 file paper.

As you can see from the illustration, this is no 'high tech' exercise, but it is essential for a layout to work. It need not take more than five or ten minutes to do, and ideally there should be several of these before you get anywhere near drawing or measuring out the plan full size. What it does do is put all your ideas on to paper where they can be seen and edited much more easily than in your mind's eye. Note that as quick as this was, I had already started making changes as I wrote, such as swapping the original bridge exit for a level crossing and adding a (highly typical) ex-LMS brake van to the possible roster of vehicles. This is by no means the finished product and the potential layout will go through many changes and substitutions before building commences.

Also note that the locomotive roster is not only small, but dedicated to the layout type. The biggest locomotive is the Q1 – this could be a C Class or a C2X instead – but this is the outside on size terms. If you want to run large locomotives

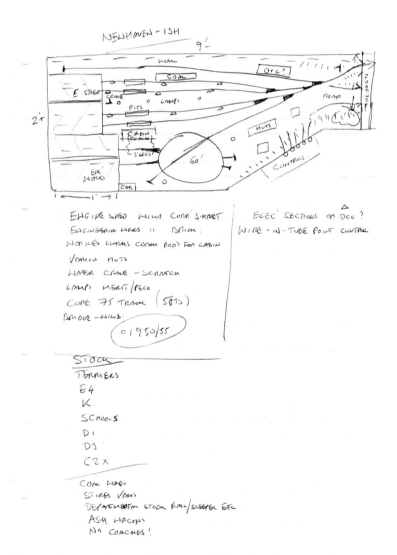

If locomotives are foremost in your modelling plan, then a motive power depot is a logical choice as it need not take up too much space. Once again, quick rough sketches firm up the idea and show you where problems may occur before you start to build.

that look at home, then sketch out a layout that visually fits (a motive power depot would be better for this in a similar space). Note also that there are rough board measurements: 9ft × 18in (2,736 × 441mm). These are what would possibly work, but it may be necessary to stretch the length to accommodate the plan. Conversely, it may be possible to compress it slightly when it is finally laid out full size.

One sticking point involves the bay platforms, as shown here. Because the point serving this has to be beyond the end of the platform, it means that you have to add at least the point length and a bit to the plan. Take the bay arrangement out of the equation and you could save yourself the best part of a foot (304mm) in length. This then becomes a compromise: do you keep the bay platform and gain operation, or take it out to gain more space? The next step is to work out how an operation sequence would run. This is really a large, separate subject, but in a nutshell, you need to establish that what you have sketched out actually does what you want it to do.

ROUGH TIMETABLES

Take another piece of paper and write out around twenty moves (about an hour's model operation). Number them one to twenty, and add twenty-four-hour clock times to them, starting with '5.55 milk train' for instance, and finishing with a 21.00h last passenger. Flesh this out a little with possible traffics, though don't get too carried away with goods traffic: a line like this would generate no more than three goods trains a day at the absolute maximum, and probably only one, and then only on Monday, Wednesday and Friday.

Within this exercise it is also worth thinking about the surroundings and making a few decisions: is it a farming area? Is it a coastal holiday area? Is there any local manufacturing? How would this affect the traffic? Hayling Island, for example, took very little goods traffic in its latter years, but the passenger train frequency was way beyond what you would first imagine due to the weight restrictions on the line and the popularity of the area with holidaymakers. All these aspects add to making your layout feel real, by giving reason for operation.

So with all this planning done, what next? At this point, if you've not done so already (still assuming 4mm scale OO), purchase a small locomotive. One on the list on the sketch would be ideal; for example, the A1X Class Terrier will fit anywhere on the Central Section, as will the E4. An M7 would be a suitable first loco to do the same branch work in the West Section, and an H Class in the East. The Q1 could have appeared anywhere except in the far west, where something more LSWR would fit better. This single locomotive may be all you need for the minute – enough to test things and to drag some rolling stock around your new layout. From this point you can build things up slowly and carefully.

So with knife or scalpel at the ready, it's on to Project One.

CHAPTER THREE

SOUTHERN REGION FREIGHT

GENERAL FREIGHT HISTORY

'The Southern didn't have any goods trains' is a comment that is often casually thrown into conversation. This is very easy to understand because, unlike the other three grouping companies, it was often thought that the Southern Region didn't have coalfields, steelworks or huge ports, which would explain the deficiency. However, this statement is, of course, completely untrue: in Southampton it had one of the country's premier ports with its own rail system, and it had its own coalfield in east Kent, which is often forgotten amongst the larger concerns of the North East, the Midlands and South Wales. Not only that, it also had naval supplies at Portsmouth and Gosport, cross-channel traffic at Newhaven, Portsmouth and the Kent ports, heavy industry around the Medway, not to mention enormous traffic-dedicated train ferries and containers at the military port at Richborough. Of course these traffic flows were nowhere near the size of, for example, the North Eastern, South Wales and Midland coalfields, but to say there was nothing is somewhat misleading.

Much of the problem stems from the pre-war publicity machine of the Southern Railway. The preferred public face of the system was a fleet of slick, efficient and increasingly electric-powered passenger trains, which took large numbers of commuters in and out of London as fast as possible. This pre-war publicity has worked, since most people see the Southern Railway and Region as an electric passenger line.

The other aspect of this problem was that to enable this fast passenger service to operate, the majority of freight workings were, if at all possible, timetabled after dark, and long after the commuting public had returned home. This meant that they weren't so visible to the travelling public, and for those of us studying and modelling the system, documentary photographs are annoyingly rare. Modern digital cameras will work quite happily in low light situations, but these were the years of film cameras when most rail enthusiasts would have had limited funds to buy high quality equipment, and the 'box Brownie' types available to the masses were all but useless once the light became dim.

Aside from these timetabling reasons, the Southern Region lacked a large fleet of modern dedicated freight locomotives, and again, although there were mid-power 0-6-0 goods engines and latterly a small number of diesel locomotives, contrary to the usual opinions, high power was often drawn from the passenger engine fleet to haul this nocturnal traffic. Even a quick glance at the figures shows that the Southern Region had a relatively small fleet of its own freight stock compared to the staggering number of wagons owned by the other three companies and regions, which amounted to hundreds of thousands. The Southern Railway was content to utilize private fleets, and continued to use the existing pre-group designs and stock until after World War II.

In broad terms there were really only two Southern Railway standard wagon designs (discounting the small numbers of specialist vehicles): a 12-ton eight-plank open wagon, and a 12-ton twelve van (which was really a slightly updated South East and Chatham Railway vehicle). Both of these wagons went through numerous build variations, but even with the more outlandish variants it is plain to see the root design. Both of these designs will be discussed later in the book.

CHANGES FOLLOWING RAILWAY NATIONALIZATION

After railway nationalization in 1948 things changed

The classic station coalyard. Note that in this photo of Corfe the staithes (coal bins) are situated in the more common position at the edge of the yard, and not the modeller's usual position against the siding. Also note the varying construction of the timber staithes.

dramatically. The system as a whole in the south, and in particular the Medway area and East Kent coast, had been particularly battered during the war, both by direct enemy attack and through overwork, and because only the most necessary repairs had been carried out. The huge fleets of privately owned open wagons had been drawn into a general 'pooling' system, and had in many cases been worked well past their useful life. This 'pooling' had effectively brought them into public ownership on a temporary basis, and now this would continue on an indefinite footing.

The trouble was that the then new British Railways did not want thousands of wagons that were first, worn out, and second, often built to non-standard designs. The Railway Clearing House (RCH) plans that took place in several stages in the first half of the twentieth century had sought to make wagon design as specified as possible using a set of pre-determined part designs. In essence this meant that wherever in the country a wagon was situated, there would be a set of dedicated parts in place to repair it on site, without it having to be moved or home repair parts sent for. This had worked, up to a point, but now with a fully nationalized system, the plan could be implemented wholesale.

The disposal numbers during the period are startling: in 1948 some 83,000 vehicles were disposed of, from which point the figures steadily increased until the 1950s peak in 1958, when 120,000 went. Even so, these numbers still didn't reach the 1960s levels, when the freight operation was once again turned on its head. The major casualties were wagons with grease-lubricated axleboxes, which were first in the firing line, but the opinion was that all short-wheelbase – under 9ft (2,736mm) – wooden wagons would have to go, to be replaced by fully braked, longer (and therefore faster) steel

TIP: USE PHOTOGRAPHS AS A BASE FOR YOUR PURCHASES

Study photographs of the area and period you are modelling, and note the type and style of wagons that seem most numerous. Use these as a base for your purchases. You will probably discover that the disposal rates took effect very quickly, and that British Railway designs are in the majority after 1955.

vehicles. This plan later (in the mid-1950s) included designing a range of wagons that could be used all over the system, using a more or less standard set of parts.

Or that was the theory, at least. Looking at this now it appears to be a plan with so many contradictions and caveats that instead of looking forwards, the design team were almost forced into hanging on to the past.

THE OPEN COAL WAGON

As far as open coal wagons were concerned, the main problem in development was a physical one: the places where coal loads originated and were heading to, had track systems that in many cases had their origins in archaic nineteenth-century working. Clearances were tight, and track curvature could be extreme compared with mainline practice. The upshot of this was that the ideal coal container throughout the country was short – generally less than 17ft (5,168mm) long – and had a comparatively short wheelbase – typically 9ft (2,736mm) or less – between axles. It was also fitted with hand-operated brakes, and was rarely more than 8ft 6in (2,584mm) high.

The practical reasons for this were that for bulk movements it had to fit under loading screens (coal shutes) for filling, and into some sort of single wagon tippler at the destination. These tipplers held the entire wagon, and either up-ended it to dispatch the load through the end flap doors, or turned the vehicle upside down in a sideways motion to empty the wagon from the top. Both of these methods obviously required the vehicle to be uncoupled from adjoining wagons, and this action provoked great resistance amongst the workforce to the introduction of any piped air or vacuum brake systems, as this would have necessitated disconnecting and connecting the pipes for each wagon to be tipped. The existing system just required a quick flip of the three-link

The standard design Southern Railway 12-ton open wagon. Although the eight-plank side was peculiar to the Southern, the general body design is common to most late nineteenth- and early twentieth-century open wagons.

The classic 'standard' BR 16-ton steel mineral wagon in typical working condition. Built in hundreds of thousands, they soon became the most numerous goods vehicle on the system, and no post-war pre-1990s layout is complete without several of these. Surprisingly not many have made it to preservation considering their numbers, and also that they were still being used in collieries into the 1990s. This is the standard design 16-tonner with a single side/double lever brake. The white stripe quickly shows at which end the end door is placed.

coupling chain by the shunter's pole – a couple of seconds' work with an experienced hand.

All this technical reasoning also needs to be viewed from the overall political position at the time: a newly elected Labour government had nationalized rail and coal industries, and the feeling amongst the workforce was that they were now better off and had more control over working practices and job security. Changing an entire set of work practices to something more automated was not so much difficult at this point as impossible, even with regard to the humble coal wagon, whose basic design in real terms had changed little in over a hundred years. What came about was a design that continued in

commercial use in the Kent collieries and all over the UK for the next forty years.

THE STEEL-BODIED COAL WAGON

During the early 1940s both the London Midland and Scottish Railway and the London and North Eastern Railway had produced all-steel wagon designs, which were the same basic dimensions as the classic wooden-bodied coal wagon. Both of these designs were a reaction to the then current Department of Transport's requirement for a more durable wagon design during hostilities. Although these designs were separate, the shape is so similar that it seems unlikely that there wasn't some sort of consultation between parties. After the war this design was adopted as the basic type to replace the wooden coal-wagon fleet. Piped brake versions were built, but not widely adopted for the reasons given above, and a simple dual hand-braked steel box with small side doors and a flap end door was set as the standard BR design.

MODELLING THE STEEL-BODIED COAL WAGON

It does appear strange that a book laying out ideas for modelling the Southern Region should start the wagon-building programme with a foreign company design, but as stated earlier, it is the typical, and not the logical, that gives the flavour. If you look at half-a-dozen photos of Southern Region pick-up freight trains from the mid-1950s, then it's quite likely that more than 50 per cent of the open wagons will be steel 16-ton mineral designs – and designs plural, because like all standard British Railways designs, no two would be alike. There were both riveted and welded bodies, fitted and unfitted, with upper side doors or not, slope-sided and 'French' (the latter had been returned after being sent to France to help with rebuilding post-war, but the European rail systems were already using much longer and faster wagon designs, and they couldn't wait to send these archaic, dumpy vehicles back).

All these were different designs in detail, but all were 16-ton minerals, and they were every-where – over a quarter of a million were built in the post-war years, many lasting into the 1980s. So the post-1950s Southern Region modeller will need 16-tonners – lots of them.

PROJECT ONE: KIT-BUILT OPEN WAGONS FOR THE SOUTHERN REGION LAYOUT

Although there are ready-to-run versions on the market, kit-building a rake or two of open coal wagons is an enjoyable modelling experience. The first example is a gentle introduction to kit build-ing, especially if you have little or no experience

of it. Most wagon kits follow the same construc-tion order, and the example is one of more than half-a-dozen 16-ton mineral wagon kits that you could choose from. Parkside Dundas produce six variants, and the most readily available is the Dapol (ex-Airfix) version, which represents the most common prototype, Diagram 108. Any will do as a first try, and here I have used a Cambrian Models kit (kit C10) of an early version built by the London & North Eastern Railway (LNER) in 1945, which was swallowed up into the BR fleet.

TOOLS REQUIRED:
- Cutting mat
- Scalpel or craft knife
- Small steel rule
- Small drills and chuck with which to hold them
- Liquid solvent such as Mek-Pak, and a small brush with which to apply it
- Needle files and sanding stick
- All-purpose adhesive such as UHU
- Blu-tack

Materials required:
- Cambrian mineral wagon kit (ref. C10)
- Transfers (Modelmaster or similar)
- Wheelsets and pinpoint bearings (Alan Gibson or similar)
- Paint

The above list of tools comprises just about as basic a toolkit as you can get for putting a kit together. In theory any kit should fall together, though that is rarely the case and most need a little fettling in the shape of removing 'flash' (excess plastic) from the parts and opening up holes in parts such as axle boxes. The set of tools described will be used throughout the book, as most of the projects include at least some plastic work. Note that the knife that is used is a very cheap, snap-off disposable, which is adequate for most work, and the sanding stick is a home-produced item (wet-and-dry type paper wrapped round a lolly stick and fixed with all-purpose adhesive). These can also be bought commercially in shops such as chemists that deal

The basic toolkit needed for most plastic wagon kits.

in nail-care items. Additional useful tools include a small engineer's square, tweezers, nail scissors and small pliers.

METHOD

First read the instructions. This may seem blindingly obvious, but read them all the way through before starting. Any kit will occasionally have alternative parts and some prototype variation, so these decisions are best made early on.

Also extra parts may be needed. For example, the Dapol and Parkside 16-tonners come with wheelsets, and the Dapol comes with transfers as well. However, the Cambrian kit has neither included so they need to be bought separately. This is frustrating if you are a beginner and want to get started quickly, but it does mean that you have choices and don't have to accept what you are given in the kit.

This kit is fairly typical of the normal building sequence. There is a flat floor to which you add the

Bearings inserted and wheelsets fitted. Note that setting the wheels parallel and level is more important than the solebar mouldings being even.

TIP: TRY A DRY RUN

Don't accept that the location marks on the floor are the best place to put them. Try a dry run, inserting the wheelsets and fixing the solebars using Blu-tack. In many cases the location marks don't allow for the slightly over-scale axle length, and the solebars end up being splayed outwards. Easing out the fixing point by half a millimetre or so each side makes sure that the solebar/axlebox assembly is vertical.

solebar parts. The top-hat type bearings are first pushed through the holes, and the solebars cleaned of any flash and stuck to the floor.

Fit one solebar, then tack the other with the wheelsets between, checking that both axles are parallel and level before fixing them solid. Do this on a completely flat surface such as a piece of glass or a kitchen worktop to make sure the unit does not rock, and that all four wheels touch the ground. It won't matter how good the final product looks if it won't stay on the track because the chassis is out of square.

Fit one side to one end and check for fit with the completed floor unit, using Blu-tack to hold the parts. Only when you are completely happy run a little solvent down the joint. Attach the remaining pair in similar fashion, and complete the box of the body around the floor, adjusting if necessary.

Brake gear, buffers and any other additional parts can now be added, according to the instructions. Very lightly sanding the face of the brake block often improves the fit against the wheel, as does sanding the face of the brake part where it joins the floor. Again, always trial fit, and don't fix permanently until you are fully satisfied that all is well and that the brake blocks are not preventing the wagon wheels from turning.

The body parts are held with Blu-tack while solvent is added.

TIP: SAND TO FIT

Most corner joints on wagon bodies will be mitred: that is, each edge is cut at 45 degrees. This is often not quite the case, however, so use the sanding stick to lightly improve this so that the corner joint is snug. Also, there are often slightly mismatched parts, particularly on older kits or at places where the mould-ing is very thin and is easily damaged. These can be filled with small pieces of plastic strip and sanded to shape when hardened off.

Any small gaps can be filled with plastic strip and filed flush when hard.

PAINTING

At the end of most kit instruction sheets there are details of paint colours and any wagon letter-ing. These are usually well researched and accurate. However, these are often the 'official' colours for the vehicle as it was 'ex-works', and not how it probably was after a couple of months in service. Therefore the modeller has choices: either follow the instruc-tion details, or do a little basic research. The advice to 'look at the prototype first' will be repeated con-stantly throughout the book – although in this case, as we cannot view the prototype in service, we can only study photographs and use common sense and reasoning. It is possible to look at preserved exam-ples, though they are by their very nature preserved to a high standard and in most cases won't represent a working wagon, which will be 'weathered'.

'Weathering' is an all-encompassing term used to describe the visual effects of outside forces on the surface of the vehicle, and not just the weather. In this case with our 16-ton coal wagon these are likely to be quite hard wear and tear, coal residue,

brake dust, corrosion and other dirt. Coal wagons lead a hard existence, and any paint on the inside surfaces would be quickly removed by the action of dropping coal in and then tipping it out again, scratching the steel surface. Add a damp outside environment, and this would quickly corrode to a light rust, which would be removed by each load of coal, only to return each time the load was emptied. So the inside of the wagon would be a light rust colour with some coal residue.

This can be suggested by first painting the entire wagon an orangey brown (Humbrol 62). This is a thin base coat and not the final surface, so there is no need for it to be neat. Then add the ex-works paint to the body sides, in this case pale grey for an unfitted (hand brakes only) wagon (Humbrol 64). Then paint the underframe an off-black, such as Humbrol 67 – not quite as stark as straight matt black.

At this juncture add the lettering, here using the Modelmaster range, mixing a mineral-wagon stripe sheet and an Eastern Region sheet. This wagon is, of course, an LNER design – bizarrely for a Southern

LEFT: **The wagon is given a sloppy coat of rust colour as a base.**

BELOW: **The completed 1945 16-ton mineral wagon.**

Region book – and so would be lettered thus even if its home base was Kent. The early company-built wagons were amalgamated with the BR fleet, so typically there would be as many 'E'- and 'M'-lettered wagons as 'B'-lettered British Railways nationalized mineral wagon stock.

Next, run a matt black colour all over the inside of the wagon using a wash technique, just enough for it to stick, but not enough for it to cover the orangey brown. Repeat this washing action on the outside using the Humbrol 67, holding the wagon upside down so that the paint runs to the top of the wagon and settles under the overhanging surfaces. This is to replicate the dust clinging to the sides, but much of it having been washed off the lower open surfaces by the rain.

Finally 'dry brush' (see box) areas of rivet detail and around the underframe with the orangey brown

TIP: PRACTISE THE DRY-BRUSH TECHNIQUE

Dry-brushing is where paint is loaded on to the brush, but then most of it is wiped off on a tissue before use. It may be worth practising this wash and dry-brush technique on an old, ready-to-run model first.

(62) already used, also brick red (70) and a touch of light brown (29) around the brakes and axle box parts.

This method can be used for all the rolling stock models in the book. There are other methods that work just as well, and extra materials such as weathering powders that you can use, but this basic paint method is reliable and gives a good basic result.

As stated earlier, there is a wide variation in 16-ton mineral wagons, so it's quite fun building up a rake of these using all the various kits in finishes

from fairly clean, like this one, to truly appalling examples with rust patches and welded repairs. Any colour photographs of coal trains from the 1950s to the 1980s will give you plenty of ideas.

MODELLING A SOUTHERN EIGHT-PLANK GENERAL MERCHANDISE WAGON

As regards pure Southern open wagons, there is one that was built in large numbers: the Diagram 1379 eight-plank general merchandise wagon. A few of these will certainly give your layout a flavour of the region. Getting on for eight thousand of these were built from 1927 to 1933, which is a large build number for the Southern Railway, and many of them passed into BR hands post-1948. By this time they had done their war service and, like many other wagons, had been upgraded from 12 to 13 tons (this wartime one-ton upgrade across the entire fleet probably did as much to hasten the demise of many wagons as did attacks from the Luftwaffe).

The basic body shape came in eight versions, including a 'stretched' 20-ton vehicle for ferry use,

The standard Southern eight-plank open wagon. Note the steel reinforcement at the lower ends to prevent damage from slipping loads.

Comparison of the 16-ton mineral (right) and the SR open, showing the shorter length of the former.

but most common was the base model with a 9ft wheelbase and Morton brakes.

Modelling is straightforward, again using a Cambrian kit as the basis. The same building methods can be used for the eight-plank as were used for the 16-ton mineral, but with one extra refinement: the corners of all wooden-planked open wagons had metal corner plates, and once the wagon body has been built, run a sanding stick or file gently over the corners to create a slightly rounded, soft edge.

These two open wagons counterbalance each other: one the boringly typical wagon that lasted from the mid-1950s to the 1980s and sets the period as post-war, and one pre-war vehicle whose unusual eight-plank design firmly sets your goods train in the Southern Region.

SCRATCH-BUILDING

The two above models are examples of straight kit-building with little or no modification. However, if you want something the kit manufacturers don't produce, the alternative is to scratch-build. This in itself is not that difficult, though the thought of it often deters the novice modeller. This is understandable, as the quality of the current ready-to-run (RTR) models is so good that even the most accomplished scratch-builder finds it hard to match the standard. That said, don't let it put you off trying: there is much to be gained from making something that is individual and personal to you.

In addition there is a 'halfway house' in the form of what is often referred to as 'kit-bashing'. This is a rather crude and not particularly descriptive term for taking a commercial kit and modifying it slightly to represent something that it was not designed to do. Modellers have been doing this for decades, and there are many articles, particularly in pre-1990s magazines, that describe this sort of model work.

TIP: LOOK OUT FOR SECOND-HAND MODEL MAGAZINES

Keep an eye out for bundles of cheap second-hand model magazines from the 1970s and 1980s at exhibitions. Discard the pages you don't want and keep the articles on kit-bashing and general model-making. Many of the kits used are still available, and the techniques described within them are still very valid today.

Taking a simple kit and adding a few details is an easy entry into scratch-building, and will give the novice confidence in part-making techniques before they take on a full scratch-build – though it's worth pointing out that it would be foolish to ignore the plethora of commercial parts that are available, such as buffers and axle boxes. No one would expect you to produce your own wheels when there are plenty of wheelsets available that can be bought relatively cheaply. This means that even a full scratch-build will only be close to 80 per cent made from raw material anyway.

MODELLING AN ASHFORD WAGON

The subject for this next project is a simple three-plank drop-side merchandise wagon built at Ashford in Kent in 1949 to BR diagram 1/16. It follows the design shape of the very similar LMS three-plank, but with several small local variations, making it firstly a typical BR vehicle, and secondly, purely Southern Region. The modifications are small, but will give you a wagon that is unique amongst all the other three-plank wagons. Following the idea

of using commercial items, it uses the very readily available Ratio Models LMS Medium Open Wagon kit (cat. 573) as the base. The extras that need to be obtained may seem like an unnecessary expense, but the spoked wheels included in the kit could be used for the SR eight-plank described above; furthermore, for those who are serious about model making, having a bundle of plastic sheet and strip material in different sizes is a pre-requisite.

PROJECT TWO: SOUTHERN-BUILT THREE-PLANK MERCHANDISE WAGON

Tools and materials required:
- Tools as listed for Project One above, plus a household needle and needle files
- Ratio Models 573 kit
- 60 × 60-thou square plastic strip, Evergreen or Slaters
- 60-thou plastic sheet (scrap)
- 1mm plastic rod
- Three-hole 12mm disc wheels to replace the kit's spoked variety
- Paint and transfers

The Ratio Models LMS three-plank wagon kit.

TIP: CONSIDER SECOND-HAND KITS

This kit and many others in the range have been produced for many years. This means that quite frequently they turn up unmade and second-hand at exhibitions. This is a good way to cut the cost, especially if you are not too confident and don't want to ruin a brand new kit. The down side is that the older versions probably won't include the high quality metal wheels and bearings that are packed with the newer kits. Check what's inside, and weigh up whether the saving really is a saving when balanced against buying new wheels.

METHOD

The first thing to do is to change the ends, which is tricky. For some inexplicable reason the Ashford works built this wagon with wooden end baulks rather than the steel angle irons that feature on all other contemporary wagons. This gives it the appearance of a wagon that was built in 1920 rather than 1949 (this may have been due to immediate post-war steel shortages). Therefore the angle irons moulded on to the ends need to be very carefully removed using a flat or D-section needle file.

Work along the planks from the side, and take your time removing both the irons and the strapping from the three planks. Then using the file again, work up from the bottom and remove the iron from the buffer beam so that all is flat. Repeat: take your time. If this takes an hour and it goes well, it will be better than trying to do it in five minutes when you may end up throwing the kit away. When all is flat, use a knife blade held sideways against a ruler on the plastic to re-cut the plank marks where the irons were, as the timber is slightly narrower. The rest of the conversion is much easier.

Add lengths of 60-thou square-section plastic over the marks left by the removal of the angle irons; then round the top edges very slightly with a file. Next, form bolt heads by 'pricking' the face of the plastic with a household needle held in a pin chuck. You are in effect making a small angled hole, but what should happen is that this will fill with paint later on, leaving the raised plastic that has been forced up to represent the bolts. This is an improvisation and the purists will object strongly, but in the smaller scales, such as 4mm, it works quite well.

Cut four small triangles of 60-thou plastic (from waste material if possible) and stick them on to the solebars. Find the positions by lining up the wagon sides and using the vertical strapping as a guide. Then make up the chassis unit following the instructions,

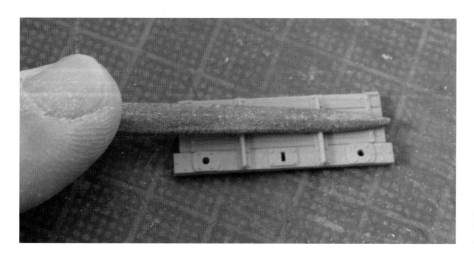

Removing the steel uprights with a needle file.

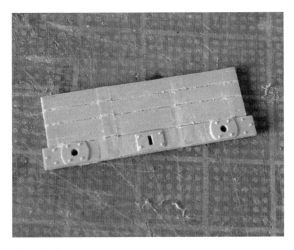

The 'flat' wagon end.

Adding rivets with a needle and pin chuck.

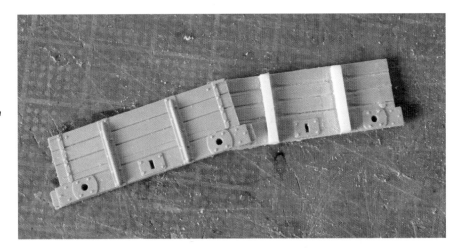

One modified end from steel angle to timber upright.

noting that in this kit the solebars are added to the side of the floor piece, and that the tops of both of these are flush. Make sure that the wagon chassis sits level and square before moving on any further.

Clean up the brake units and slim down the brake shoes in width slightly as with the previous projects; then stick the units to the floor in line with the outside edge of the wheels. When the joins are hardened, add a length of 1mm diameter plastic rod (or brass wire) between the brake units adjacent to the pivot marks. Note that one side has a 'cam' arrangement.

One of the differences between the London, Midland Region-built and the Southern-built wagons is the 'thickening up' of the headstock. This is easily

Triangular fillets added to the solebar.

Floor and solebars fitted together.

Brakes added with a micro-rod cross-rod.

modelled by adding a 60-thou square strip. Rest the strip against the back of the head-stock, and run some solvent through the joint; let it harden for a while, then trim off the excess. Repeat this with all four corners.

Finish assembling the wagon body and add it to the chassis. Finally add the strapping at the edge of the ends as shown, and the bolt heads using the technique demonstrated above. The kit can now be finished in the same way as the two above.

The whole process is not 100 per cent accurate, but what it does do is give you a little more experience in kit-bashing, and a vehicle that not only conveys the spirit of the

BELOW LEFT: **Buffer-beam extension added from plastic strip.**

BELOW RIGHT: **Close-up showing the 'thickened up' buffer beam.**

The completed Ashford-built three-plank merchandise wagon.

TIP: KEEP SPARE PARTS

Keep a small margarine tub-type box handy for all the spare parts that are left on the kit sprues. For instance the Ratio kit will leave a vacuum cylinder and four pipes, and these should be kept for later use for possibly upgrading an unfitted wagon kit to a vacuum-fitted version, at no extra cost to you.

Ashford three-plank wagon, but will also give you a very individual wagon that is just a little different to all the other three-plankers in the train. In addition it will give a conversation piece at an exhibition or club meeting.

A NOTE ON COUPLINGS

You will have noticed that no couplings have been added to the above three wagons. This is because the owner of the layout for which they were destined had not decided which system to use. All the kits come with provision for Tri-ang type hook and bar couplers, which can be altered to fit any of the current commercial similar items – though couplers tend to be one area that is quite personal to most modellers.

SOUTHERN RAILWAY COVERED GOODS WAGONS

In 1929 the Southern Railway produced the first of its closed vans (correctly termed 'covered goods wagons'). These were built on 'Railway Clearing House' (RCH) designed underframes, and although they were designed at the Lancing carriage works, the bodies were a close match to the earlier South

Fully fitted SR ventilated van ('XP' denotes it is cleared for running in fitted express trains).

East and Chatham Railway vans but without the bottom flap doors. The original batches were wooden bodies on a 9ft wheelbase frame, which was increased to 10ft (3,040mm) for later builds. The bodies were iron-framed with planked sides and ends; in later batches these planks were a mix of wide and narrow widths in order to save on construction costs. By the end of World War II the planking was replaced with the even cheaper option of plywood sheeting, a practice that British Railways continued with the final batches that were built in 1949.

As with the 'standard' eight-plank open wagon covered earlier, the SR produced many variants of this standard design, including refrigerator and fruit vans with no ventilators, to meat vans with seven vents stacked vertically at the centre of each end. The standard two-vent variety was very long-lived, lasting in some cases until the end of steam and late into the 1970s in departmental use.

PROJECT THREE: BUILDING THE SR 12-TON PLYWOOD SHEATHED VAN

Materials and tools required:
- Ratio SR plywood van, cat: 593
- 20 × 10-thou plastic strip
- 40 × 20-thou plastic strip (optional)
- 20-thou plastic rod
- Couplers of choice
- Sanding stick
- Needle files
- Craft knife or scalpel
- Small drill bits
- Solvent and brush
- Paint and transfers

The modeller is very well served, with Ratio models providing three variant kits of planked and plywood vans in 4mm. All are on the standard Ratio 10ft wheelbase underframe, the same moulding as was used with the three-plank wagon dealt with earlier. It would, however, be fairly straightforward to swap this with a 9ft long example in the case of the earlier planked kits if so desired. In fact the enthusiastic

modeller could probably produce a dozen variants with these three kits by changing underframes, wheel styles and/or brake gear. In general, wagons are either a modeller's minefield or a kit-basher's delight, depending on your point of view, as once in service all were subject to various repairs and upgrades; so if creating individual wagons is to your taste, then the world really is your oyster.

METHOD

The kit used for this project is the later plywood version, Diagram 1452, and is built here more or less as the instructions, with a couple of easy additions, which will make it your own. These are detailed as the build progresses with a couple of suggestions of further upgrades that are not carried out in this instance.

The kit is supplied with brass bearings. These are a tight fit in the axle boxes so ideally need to be drilled out with a 2mm drill bit. The best way to do this is by hand and not with any powered drill as the operation needs great care. What you don't want to do is drill all the way through, but just enough for the bearing to drop in. The bearings can then have a drop of solvent run around the edge, which softens the plastic just enough to 'grab' the brass.

The solebar assembly can now be cut from the sprue, and the pair fitted to the edges of the floor piece. Here the fitted brake version is being built so the V hangers are retained on both sides, and the axle-box tie-bar is also kept. The tie-bar was added to wagons to support the axle assemblies and take the outward force of the vacuum braking systems. Be aware that this section of the solebar piece is exceptionally fragile, and if you manage to remove it from the sprue without breaking it, then you'll have done very well – if it survives the whole kit build it will be even better. I have to admit that here the item was broken umpteen times and re-fixed in order to keep the kit as original as possible. Ideally the tie-bar should be replaced with a length of 20 × 40-thou plastic strip, or better still use thin brass or nickel silver.

The rest of the underframe and brake parts can be assembled following the kit instructions, but with the addition of a length of plastic rod between the V hangers and the brake cylinder.

The kit comes with separate door parts, which could be very useful if the van were to be used as a static model with open doors. For instance, if the final British Railways period was modelled the van could be set as ex-departmental use and parked up at the end of a siding as a store, with the doors open and weathered accordingly. The doors should be cleaned up and fitted; note that the handles should be in the lower half.

The ends require the backs to be sanded flush, taking off any flash (seen at the top) and the lugs that are behind the buffer housings. The two vents can be added as shown.

Gently opening out the axle-bearing holes.

Brass bearing cups fitted.

Underframe completed with vacuum cylinder.

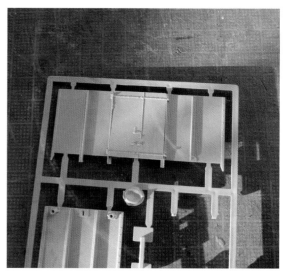

Doors added to the sides while still on the sprue.

As pointed out earlier, it was often the vents that gave the various different models their outward difference, and it does not take much effort to produce extra vent parts from a piece of 40-thou plastic sheet, cut to size and filed to shape. Most of the later prototype vents were made from pressed steel and had a horizontal ridge near the lower edge. This was to add strength, though it's hard to ascertain how much, if any pressure would be applied on something mounted 10ft in the air. Photos cer-

tainly don't suggest any damage occurring. These ridges can be represented by adding small lengths of 20 × 10-thou strip, as shown. While the ends are being worked on, run a 0.8mm drill bit through the buffer housings by hand to clear the hole. It's easier to do it at this juncture rather than when the van is built up.

The sides and ends can now be assembled as pairs. Note that it is not possible to make up the entire body and drop it over the floor due to the

File the protrusions marked flat.

Vents added with plastic strip ridge.

Lead sheet weight is doubly secured with scrap plastic.

extended bracing on the sides and the inside protrusions on the door frames. Weight should now be added. As there is plenty of available space there are several options: fill the box with wood, a large steel nut stuck to the floor, or as here, some redundant lead roofing sheet. The probability is that once the roof is on and stuck down, whatever the weight used will come adrift, so lock it in place with off-cuts of sprue from the kit, which should be stuck to the sides and floor with solvent.

The roof can now be fixed, as can the buffers and coupling hooks. Note that a sloppy first coat of paint has already been applied.

ABOVE: **Coupling hook and metal buffers added.**

Complete 12-ton ventilated van.

The van can now be painted. The basic post-war colour was what the railways called 'bauxite', a varied shade of red/brown that fairly quickly faded and in time pealed from the plywood. A visit to any preserved line will give you an idea of how poor this paint colour is for robustness under ultra-violet light. The roofs of the vans were covered in a dark grey sheet material called 'Rubberoid'.

Aside from noting the small problems with the chassis, this is an excellent kit for the steam age Southern modeller. Its strength also lies in how adaptable it is to be converted, either by changing underframe details, vents, wheels or buffers, or even the extreme conversion of representing the pent-roofed version, which was actually a planked van entirely clad in Rubberoid, giving it a smooth surface and a suggestion of garden shed. Any of the excellent books on Southern wagons will give you plenty of ideas for further upgrades and kit-bashing.

SOUTHERN REGION NON-PASSENGER ROLLING STOCK

The grey area between goods and passenger rolling stock is one that not too many modellers care to explore, especially not the novice. It's very easy to split the two types of passenger stock neatly down the middle – one for human traffic, and the other for other more personal goods such as luggage or parcels. This sidelining by the modeller may be a little short sighted, as there is much to be gained from the study and modelling of this grey area. In these days of travelling light and a 'compact hand luggage only' attitude that most of us are used to with modern airline travel, it's easy to forget that much of the steam railways' cargo was not only the human form sitting on a seat, but the huge amount of personal possessions that people carried with them.

A glance at any platform photo taken before the

Personal luggage was often piled up on platform trolleys.

mid-1960s will show that people certainly did not travel light. Large voluminous trunks of all shapes would be left in piles unattended on the platform or on barrows, usually accompanied with a paper label or a tied cardboard tag with the owner's name and home address and possibly the destination. Today for security reasons we and the carrier would be alarmed at total separation from our luggage, but only fifty years ago it was quite usual for the traveller to 'send luggage in advance' or to instruct 'luggage to follow'. And these flimsy pieces of paper were the key to its correct journey.

Unthinkable now is the prospect of travelling from London to Dorset for a fortnight's holiday on a Saturday, only to stand in the clothes you are wearing until the rest of your attire arrived on Sunday or Monday on the next suitable train, delivered to your hotel by private or rail-operated carrier. And yet that is exactly what happened. Of course, due to the amount and size of the luggage there was often no space available within the passenger compartments, so from the railway's earliest days luggage vans were attached to busy services, or run as a separate train to and from holiday destinations.

Having to be attached to possibly fast-moving passenger trains meant that the humble short-wheelbase goods vans, like the last project example above, soon became unsuitable for all but the lightest and slowest of trains; therefore all railways introduced passenger luggage vans that were express-train rated, with a long wheelbase and vacuum braked. These designs were often long lived, possibly due to the fact that although the mileage was great, the treatment was perhaps a little more forgiving.

The subject for the following project falls under the umbrella of luggage van, and yet its history is somewhat more involved. Along with belongings in trunks, passengers – or more accurately, wealthy passengers – often required their personal road vehicles to be transported with them. This again led the railways, from as early as the mid-nineteenth century, to develop specialized vehicles to carry 'carriages'. These were originally just flat trucks to which the road vehicle was strapped, but by the end of the nineteenth century these basic vehicles had developed roofs. The Southern Railway's constituent companies all built carriage trucks, but when

Southern PMV in use as a store van in the 1980s.

PMV 'preserved' 2015.

the time came for the Southern Railway to build its own, it again looked to a South East and Chatham Railway (SECR) design, which it closely replicated in two basic but similar designs.

The initial design was similar to the SECR van but with a pair of cupboard-type doors at each end. This initial batch was coded 'general utility van' (GUV), but further builds of this type were coded 'covered carriage' (COVCAR) because road vehicles could be end loaded through the cupboard doors and run over a drop-down flap that covered the van's buffers.

A further similar luggage van design emerged without the end doors, and was coded 'parcels and miscellaneous van' (PMV). This coding remained under British Rail, but COVCAR disappeared, to be replaced, in a strange twist of historical terminology, by the 'covered carriage truck' (CCT). The term 'utility van' has clung on, and all these vans are often referred to as a group in this way, with only the end doors defining the difference.

The GUV/CCT/PMV vans were incredibly long-lived, lasting in service well into the 1970s even into rail blue livery, and lasting into the 1980s as departmental stores vans. This has meant that many have survived into preservation, and most heritage lines

have at least one. Under British Railways, further batches of Southern CCTs were constructed, again using plywood for the side panels (but not any of the doors), and it is this later 1950s version that is the subject of the next project.

PROJECT FOUR: BUILDING THE 1950s COVERED CARRIAGE TRUCK (CCT)

Although the instructions for the kit do work adequately, the order here has been changed slightly to ease the assembly and to leave space for the slight additions to the kit. The tools and materials are much the same as for the SR 12-ton van detailed above.

THE ROOF AND CHASSIS

To get it out of the way and off the work-bench area, tackle the roof first and add the shell vents where marked on the underside. These marks need to be drilled through, however, the marks are not all that clear: the measurements from each end are 19mm and 49mm. Make sure that the points of the vents face to the side of the roof. Give the whole roof a light coat of dark grey paint, and put it to one side to dry.

First add the roof vents.

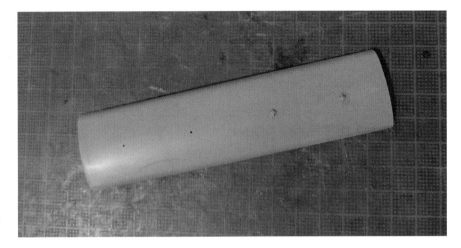

*BELOW: **Opening out the axle boxes with a 2mm drill.***

The axle boxes need to be drilled as with the van at 2mm diameter, but they also benefit from being dished with a larger (here, 3mm) household drill. This just requires a few light turns to soften the edge. Then add the bearings as before. One V hanger needs to be removed from one solebar, indicated by the knife point in the photo.

The solebars can now be added to the floor using Blu-tack to temporarily fix them while they are joggled to get the axles parallel (though here the close-up camera lens makes this look anything but). It's worth noting that once the wheelbase of plastic goods vehicles increases, so does the risk of longitudinal twist in the chassis frame.

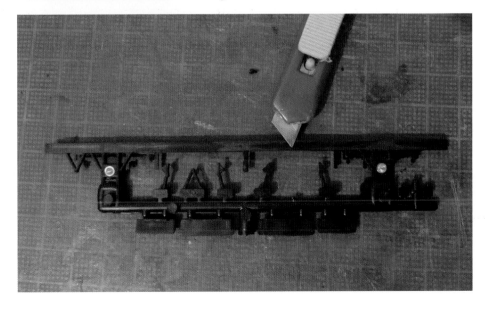

Remove the V hanger from one side at this point.

Trial fit the solebars and wheelsets, and make sure that all is free running and parallel before adding solvent.

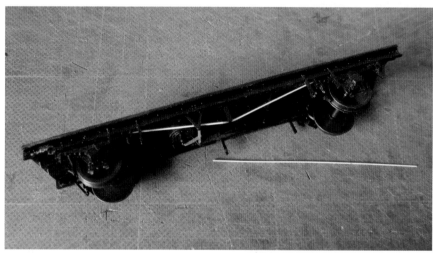

1mm rod is bent before threading it behind the post and the V hanger.

Although it has not been done here, this is one place where an axle compensation unit could help to keep all four wheels on the track. This is a method used by the modellers working in the finer 4mm scale standard track gauges of 18.2mm and 18.83mm, though even in OO gauge this may help with the longer vehicles. The compensation units (known as 'rocking W irons') are usually made from etched brass and are often available from exhibitions put on by the finescale modelling societies.

Add the vacuum cylinder and the operating rod as shown, and assemble the sides and ends in pairs as for the short-wheelbase van above.

Cut two 76mm lengths of the 1mm rod supplied and gently bend them in the centre. The rod represents the truss rods and fits behind all the solebar protrusions, and centres around the small circular knob on the rear of the central vertical 'queen post'.

BODYWORK

Run a 2mm drill through the buffer shanks to clear. The buffers supplied are not quite right and could be replaced with a set with a square base-plate (see the PMV photo at the end of the previous section). If the kit buffers are used a small amount of plastic needs to removed from the drop-down doors on the ends to enable the round plate to sit flat. Failure to do this will result in a decidedly droopy set of buffers.

The buffer holes need to be opened out with a 2mm drill.

BELOW: *The bottom of the flap needs to be carved slightly to take the back plate of the buffer.*

meant that the paint soon faded. It's worth looking at some prototype photos of the period that you are modelling as the CCT/PMV colours seem to vary wildly in service, with the early reds lasting right into the 1980s in some cases.

THE UNDERSIDE DETAILS

While the paint is drying the footsteps can be worked on. The kit lower steps have a small ridge, which goes at the top. However, a study of the prototype shows that most of the time this ridge is

At this point it is probably worth giving the body a base coat of paint. The ply CCTs were British Railways maroon from the outset, with the end doors painted plain black. This presumably was to match with the new general British Railways carriage livery of the time. In later repaints the vans again appeared in various shades of green to match the shift of the carriage colours, but this time the ends were painted the same colour as the sides.

Don't just take the official colour line as being accurate. Different local paint shops painted different shades, and this, coupled with the long service of many vans and long periods between repaints,

File a gap in the vertical part of the steps.

The gap was there to allow access to the J hanger.

split. This was probably done to allow access to the J hanger on the spring, which sits immediately behind. It is of course the work of seconds to replicate this using a flat needle file. These can now be fitted to the step struts as shown.

The end view of the van shows all too clearly the rod between the brake shoe assemblies. This is not included in the kit but can be run up very easily from 0.5mm (20-thou) plastic rod, which is sprung between all four of the shoes and fixed with solvent.

One other quite noticeable item when viewed from the end is the linkage from the handbrake. This activates a set of rodding that runs the entire length of the underside of the van. This rodding is largely hidden from normal angles, so has been omitted here, but the initial linkage is worth putting in. Again this is not allowed for in

Add 0.5mm rod between the brakes.

Triangular part made from microstrip.

Triangle fitted and rod added.

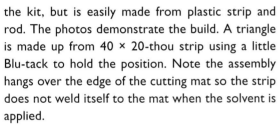

the kit, but is easily made from plastic strip and rod. The photos demonstrate the build. A triangle is made up from 40 × 20-thou strip using a little Blu-tack to hold the position. Note the assembly hangs over the edge of the cutting mat so the strip does not weld itself to the mat when the solvent is applied.

Note also the pencil mark at the right as a reminder as to where the bottom edge is. This edge sits on the van floor against one of the longitudinal runners. When the triangle is set it can be added to the van and a length of rod added between it and the brake handle, which is included in the kit. If you wanted to go to modelling extremes you could add all the brake yokes and the pull rods. These are detailed in drawings that can be accessed on the internet and in several wagon books. There are also a couple of companies who offer etched brass parts for those modellers who wish to go just that little bit further, though most will be content with the peripheral detailing covered here.

WINDOWS

Once the window glazing has been added to the sides there is one other detail to add. All the CCT/PMVs usually had safety bars over the inside of the windows to stop luggage pushing against the glass. Again these bars are not in the kit, but can be added

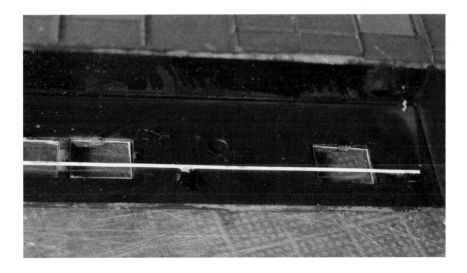

Long strip added behind the windows.

The finished CCT.

by using 40 × 20-thou strip once again. The bars were originally painted white, but this looks a bit stark, so paint a couple of lengths of strip a pale grey, then add them full length behind the windows. This may look a little wasteful, but it ensures that the horizontal bar line stays consistent along all four window openings.

THE FINISHED CCT

This build description may appear over-critical of the kit, but this is not intentionally so: the plastic mouldings are excellent, and it will make up perfectly well as it stands. All that has been done is to add a few simple details to give the impression of a finely tuned piece of rolling stock for very little extra effort.

The Southern Region was primarily a passenger-driven line, and no contemporary layout would be complete without a few long-wheelbase luggage vans – possibly a whole train of them in different livery states and conditions. As with the 12-ton goods van, the slight variants are many, and it would be possible to add and subtract parts and finish in different painting styles.

TIP: CREATING THE AUTHENTIC LOOK

Photos from the 1960s onwards show PMVs and CCTs in various liveries, as the painting did not always follow the up-to-date style. For an authentic look mix maroon, green and possibly rail blue (from 1965 onwards) in the same train. If your layout is large, then a mix of these four-wheel vans and the longer bogie versions (available from Ratio Models) could make up rakes of dedicated parcel or newspaper trains. These ran between London and major points and ports within the system for onward distribution. These would, of course, be run at night on the outward trip, but would probably return in the early daylight hours. The research of some of these specialist timetabling flows is fascinating and helps the modelling experience, but time wise it often draws the modeller away from the physical act of making things.

CHAPTER FOUR

SOUTHERN REGION LOCOMOTIVES

WHAT LOCOMOTIVE?

In the introductory chapter I pointed out that the modeller of the Southern Region is very well served in the twenty-first century with regard to locomotives and rolling stock, especially in the popular scale of 4mm (OO). However, this abundance of riches can confuse the novice, who may be tempted to buy up everything with a Southern Railway/Region tag on it. Of course there is nothing wrong with this approach and the model manufacturers will be thrilled if you do this, but as with the advice on layout planning, a little forethought before purchasing goes

a long way. As always there can be a down side, and here it is a question of timing. The shift to very high quality products has also introduced the 'batch production' system that the Americans have used for years. This works well there, as most prototype American railroads use (in very loose terms) standard units from companies such as EMD or Alco, so in a lot of cases it is only livery detail that is different; the same or similar locomotive classes can be found from Alaska to Florida.

The situation in the UK is slightly different, in that a model will appear in one livery, then be produced in a second, and may then disappear from

Preserved ex-LSWR 'long frame' M7 kept at Swanage MPD. The front footplate was extended on later batches to accommodate an air reservoir behind the buffer beam.

TIP: BUYING ROLLING STOCK ITEMS

If you have a rolling stock item that is a 'must have', it may be better to buy it when you see it and don't expect it to be around forever.

TIP: LOOK OUT FOR SECOND-HAND LOCOMOTIVES

Keep a sharp eye out for second-hand or discounted locomotives at model railway exhibitions that may have a future use, or which you can use to practise new modelling techniques.

the market for a while. This means that your careful long-term purchasing plan is flawed, because by the time you decide to buy the model, it may well have disappeared from the shops. Specifically a case in point relevant to our subject is the Hornby M7 Class in BR black, which was only available for a short time and now is quite rare, despite being only a fairly recent production. Even in 7mm scale (O), where you would expect batch runs to be long, in fact they are likewise short, and even the kit producers can come and go quite quickly.

So the reality is that you have to find a balance between planning carefully, and buying models when they are first produced.

THE HORNBY (EX-DAPOL) A1X CLASS TERRIER

With all that aside, the first thing the novice Southern Region modeller should do is obtain a good all-round workhorse locomotive that is happy on both passenger and freight work. The Hornby (ex-Dapol) A1X-Class Terrier is a prime choice. Yes, they were Central Section based, but both the LSWR and SECR bought Terriers from the LBSCR, so there is a slim excuse for using one in the east or west. Another good all-rounder from the trade would be the Q1 Class 0-6-0, which is equally at home on passenger or freight. For the late period modeller the Class 33 (D6500) diesel is about as perfect a dual purpose locomotive as you could find, followed by the electro-diesel Class 73, both of which are available ready to run in 4mm scale.

But is this modelling? Well, yes and no. No, in that you have purchased something that will run straight out of the box and which is made by someone else, but yes, in that there are always compromises in any ready-to-run model. The model manufacturers have to leave things off for cost reasons, and to some extent, ease of packaging. This is where the modelling lies – in the detailing. The following project outlines the upgrading of a Hornby A1X Class 'Terrier' with a small amount of work that could be applied in similar fashion to any small steam locomotive in 4mm scale.

THE A1X CLASS TERRIER

BRIEF CLASS HISTORY

The William Stroudley-designed A1 0-6-0T was first produced in 1872 and has become somewhat of an icon, possibly because of its diminutive size, or because it worked (or still works) some of the best loved small branch lines, both long closed and currently preserved. Fifty locomotives were built, numbered 35 to 84, and despite the common assumption that they are a branch line loco, they were in fact primarily designed to work South London commuter traffic, hauling fixed rakes of four-wheel coaches.

This initial workload was quickly overtaken by the need for heavier and longer trains requiring a larger locomotive. Although the A1s were ideally suited to their original brief, with good haulage for their size and sporting comparatively large 4ft-diameter driving wheels, their days were quickly numbered, and scrapping began as early as 1901 when eleven locomotives were disposed of. What saved the class was the realization that income could be generated by the sale of the excess numbers to independent lines and industrial concerns, and also the new deployment of 'motor trains' for coastway services, where the A1s were coupled to, or often between, one or two LBSCR 'balloon' coaches.

In the years leading up to World War 1, alterations were carried out: primarily the removal of condensing pipes, the temporary change to a 2-4-0 configuration for two of the class, and from 1911 sixteen of the class were re-boilered. In cosmetic terms this added a few inches to the boiler length and required a smokebox saddle, the loss of the wing plates, and reclassification from A1 to A1X.

At this point developments became more complicated, and further alterations were specific to each locomotive: coal rails were added to some, and in the case of the Isle of Wight-based locomotives, the back of the bunkers was extended and the rear toolbox was discarded. The class was retained by the Southern Railway in 1924 and subsequently by British Railways in 1948, mainly because it could be used on weight-sensitive lines. The last A1X remaining in mainline service were withdrawn in 1963, ninety-one years after construction, though several remain in working order on preserved lines.

MODELLING IDEAS

There have been kits available for the Terrier in 4mm scale since the 1960s. The Keyser (Ks) and Westward items still turn up unbuilt on rummage stands. These are fundamentally accurate, and if you wish to model one of the more radical variants, a white-metal kit is probably the most forgiving way of doing it. In 7mm scale there have been brass kits from Albion Models and Roxey Mouldings among others, as well as more recently a ready-to-run version from Dapol. In 3mm scale a run of brass etches is occasionally available via the 3mm Society, and in N scale there is again a model from Dapol.

Hornby (ex-Dapol) Terrier as supplied.

To go with all the above 4mm items are etched nickel-silver chassis kits from Branchlines, Comet and South East Finecast. If you wished to go for the unusual 2-4-0T version with the 2ft 9in-diameter leading wheels, then one of these and a drill would be a fair place to start – although these had been long returned to 0-6-0 configuration by the start of World War II.

The 4mm Dapol/Hornby offering is the main subject, as it is probably the one that most people can obtain. It will work straight out of the box, but can be 'polished'. The photo on page 57 shows the ready-to-run model, but with the included extension ring added. This is in essence a 2mm-wide piece of plastic that drops in behind the smokebox door moulding to lengthen the boiler to the A1X dimensions. Condensing pipes and a solid coal rail part are included with the loco. These are not appropriate

for 32636, which was (and still is) a fairly unadorned A1X, and is more or less all right as it looks, except for the extra sandboxes.

The original shape bunker is correct for this number, whereas in the other British Railways' numbered Terriers from Dapol/Hornby the bunker needs to be extended up or at the back, and changes need to be made to the sandbox. This can be done with a little plastic sheet, or alternatively Golden Arrow Models make a resin part, which is a possible option when weighed against the cash/time equation.

The Hornby model is an excellent way to obtain a late period BR Terrier, which is, track gauge excepting, fairly accurate. Type the 'Terrier' into an internet search engine and add the locations of Newhaven, Hayling Island or Tenterden, and you will find enough photos to give you all the visual information you'll need.

Terrier with short bunker, coal rails and lower sandboxes.

TIP: LAYOUT IDEAS

The layout ideas based around a Terrier are numerous. Hayling Island is an obvious choice, as the Terrier was the only post-grouping motive power permitted on the branch due to the Langstone Harbour bridge weight restriction, but the last days of the Kent & East Sussex line is an overlooked idea, giving a very compact set of trains and track plans with the Terriers handling a few British Railways wagons and an ex-SECR coach or two. This would give light railway charm without the need for all the usual pre-war period excuses to run all the wacky rolling stock that light railways are renowned for.

This is a scenario that few choose, but if etched brass and white-metal kits are not for you, then you can still use plastic rolling stock and successfully create the Colonel Stephens light railway feel. (Colonel H.F. Stephens was owner and operator of a collection of small independent lines which were known for their use of poor quality, ancient, second-hand rolling stock.) Other scenarios would be the Newhaven harbour branch or Brighton locomotive works, where one British Railways Terrier was painted in the pre-grouping livery of the LBSCR's 'improved engine green', which was actually mustard yellow.

PROJECT FIVE: DRESSING THE HORNBY (EX-DAPOL) A1X CLASS TERRIER

The Hornby Terrier was first produced by Dapol in 1986, so not only is it a tried and tested model, but it has been produced in a variety of liveries and is freely available second-hand. This is a critical point for the novice, who may be nervous about taking

saws and drills to a brand new model: it is far less intimidating to hack into something that is pre-loved and half the price.

Tools required:
• Small drills and a pin chuck
• Needle files
• Sharp craft knife or scalpel
• Model filler such as Squadron
• UHU and superglue

Materials required:
• 20-thou black plastic sheet
• Soft 0.5mm diameter wire
• 1mm diameter plastic rod
• 2mm diameter plastic rod
• 10–15-thou white plastic sheet or similar
• Staples
• Locomotive crew
• Paint

TIP: STUDY YOUR SUBJECT BEFORE CUTTING

Read through this section thoroughly before tackling the cutting, and study as many prototype photographs of each area so that you are aware of what goes where, and what the final finished shape should be.

SANDBOX CHANGES

The main problem with 32636 is the sandboxes. The LBSCR moved some Terrier sandboxes to below the footplate and further forward with filler lids in front of the smokebox. The Hornby model compromises and gives you boxes both below and above, joined with the front wheel splashers as originally sited. The first and major job is to remove these. This takes a certain amount of courage, but just take your time and work slowly through it.

TIP: WORKING ON A NEW MODEL

If you are working on a brand new model make sure it is run in and thoroughly tested before you attempt any of the conversion work. Just one single modification will void any manufacturer's guarantee you have.

Remove the body, and put the chassis to one side. Remove both buffer beams by gently pulling, and if you wish, paint them red to take away the shine of the plastic. Drill a series of small holes all around the sandbox inside the line you want to finish at. Carefully join these holes with a sharp knife and remove the part. This is fiddly, and you will probably need to work from the outside and the inside of the body moulding. Gently file the cut marks back to the finished line. At this point as you stare at your mutilated Terrier you will be wondering why you started this.

Repeat with the other side. Cut a small piece of black plastic sheet (around 6–7mm square), curve it between your fingers and fit it over the hole at the top of the splasher. This will most probably take a few attempts to get right, and considerable cutting and shaping before you are happy to attach it with solvent. Again, really take your time and make sure it's as good a fit as you can get.

Build up a layer of filler in the remaining hole using a cocktail stick or matchstick. Support it with an old piece of Blu-tack on the inside, tearing it away afterwards. When this is fully dry, shape and carve the

*ABOVE: **Sandbox with pencilled cut line.***

*RIGHT: **Sandbox removed by drilling and cutting.***

Slab of plastic added and filler roughly shaped.

filler into the shape of the smokebox saddle using a round needle file. When this is completely shaped and dry, drill a 1mm hole in the saddle.

* WARNING: The next part requires the use of a naked flame and for plastic to be burnt. This will give off noxious fumes and is a fire hazard, and should only be carried out in a well-ventilated outdoor area. If you are at all unsure about this, please find an alternative method.

Take a full length of 1mm plastic rod and using a match, set the end of the rod alight for two to three seconds; then quickly extinguish it, turning the rod so that a dropped ball is formed from the melted plastic. When cool, cut a short length and fix it into the pre-drilled hole. Add a sliver of 2mm plastic rod on each side of the footplate over the lower sandboxes to represent the raised filler caps. Finally give the whole area a coat of Tamiya XF black paint.

ABOVE: **Plastic rod with melted end.**

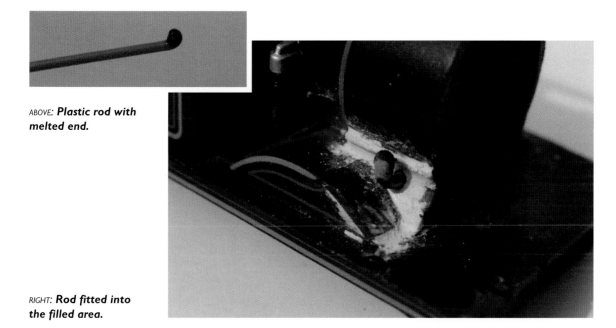

RIGHT: **Rod fitted into the filled area.**

Tank vents removed and the holes filled.

The whistle should be removed, the hole filled and the whistle re-sited 3mm further back.

TANK TOP MODIFICATIONS

Remove the two tank dome vents and fill the holes. Likewise remove the whistle, fill the hole that is left, and drill a new hole 3mm nearer to the cab. Fix the whistle into this hole.

CAB INTERIOR

At this point unclip the cab moulding by pushing the three pegs underneath. Very carefully lever off the glazing piece: this is quite fragile, so don't force it. Then run a thin wash of sand-coloured paint over the upper areas of the cab interior, and paint the

*ABOVE: **The cab painted sand colour.***

2678 again showing the rear cab detail.

handle red. This should only be a thin wash of paint – let the black bleed through. In service, cabs were not particularly clean, so you'd only have to dirty it. The black is there anyway, so make use of it.

The brake lever is far too high as it is given to you. For some reason this plug-in part has not been designed to match with the gear-wheel bulge in the footplate. The best you can do is to pull it out, cut the plug off and sand back as far as you dare, creating a 'flat' at the foot of the ratchet. Then reattach it with solvent. Touch in the backhead detail with a brush of brass paint and reattach the cab.

EXTRA PIPEWORK

The Westinghouse pump is supplied devoid of pipework, and as can be seen from the photo, there is quite a lot of it. You can take this detailing as far as you wish, but a compromise is feed pipes at top and bottom. Pipe can be made from thin soft wire such as florists' wire (as used on this model), 5amp fuse wire or single-strand telephone cable; run a length from a hole in the front of the bottom cylinder into the footplate, and another from the top cylinder over the top of the tank into a drilled hole between the tank and boiler.

The same wire can be used to create a pipe run from the back of the tank filler, curving round the boiler and down between the frames on each side; fix it with superglue.

Two lengths of 1mm plastic rod should be bent up, using hot water to soften it (a cup of hot coffee will do this more than adequately), and then fitted through two holes in the boiler top; they should be only lightly ten-

Lowered and painted brake handle.

Westinghouse pump detail.

New tank-top pipework.

sioned on to the cab front (see the ratchet photo for the hole position). The joint on the bend can be suggested by a drop of UHU. This is an improvisation, but once the whole thing is painted it blends into the loco as a whole. The pipes that you've run down the front of the tank can now be extended to the back with further pieces that join with the UHU 'joint'. The join – or lack of it – in the tank pipes will be masked by the tank filler.

When all is dry, paint with Tamiya XF1 and touch in the whistle and uprights in brass.

Note that I have kept all this work fairly non-technical. You don't necessarily need to know all the

detailed workings of a steam engine to accomplish what is purely aesthetic detailing – you just need to look. What you can do at this point if you wish, is to clutter the tank top with fire irons and oil cans. I can't stress enough that these are all suggestions, and the first thing to do in any conversion work is to study prototype photos: look and copy.

LAMP IRONS AND FINAL DETAILS

One of the most noticeable features about 32636 is the extended lamp irons. Refit the buffer-beam mouldings and file a 'flat' at the rear of each one. Drill a small hole and insert a length of straight-

Rear of the buffer housing filed flat to take the new lamp iron.

Staple lamp iron.

Smokebox top detail.

ened office staple, leaving 9mm protruding. Then add a tiny length of microstrip in front of this with superglue to represent the original short lamp iron. Repeat on all four buffers. Then using the same technique, add another short iron over the smoke-box door. Finally paint them all black.

Using a standard office hole punch, cut out a few headcode discs from thin (10–15 thou) plastic sheet, and attach them to the front of the lamp irons to suit. Add two crew members to the cab and some coal to the bunker, and finally add the vacuum pipes included with the model to the buffer beam.

Long-bunkered Terrier at Tenterden in the pouring rain.

AN ECONOMY-BASED REWORKING

It has to be said that this is a very economy-based reworking, and there is more you could do – a better casting for the Westinghouse pump, for instance, or a new cast white-metal or brass smokebox dart. However, this method will give you a more lifelike Terrier for what is only a few pence worth of materials, and possibly scrap materials at that. The point of the exercise is to encourage the novice modeller to take on the project of reworking a relatively cheap, ready-to-run commercial OO model.

SUMMARY

The basic methods outlined above can be expanded to upgrade any similar OO steam engine, and for that matter much is transferable to diesel and electrics as well. However good they are – and the current crop is extremely good – there are always flimsy details such as lamp irons that are hard to add at the manufacturing point of the plastic body, and there is always something to be added, if only a driver, fireman and a little coal in the bunker. The A1X Terrier makes a good starting point for practising this type of upgrade because there is so much information available in books and on the internet, and because it was so well photographed when in service due to its link to popular holiday destinations.

At this point it would be logical to have a section on kit-built locomotives, but if you, like most, are working in 4mm/OO scale, then it hardly seems worth the effort. At the time of writing almost all the major classes have been produced ready to run, so unless your calling is kit-building, then the time is probably better spent keeping your eye out for reasonably priced, ready-to-run locomotives of your choice, and gently upgrading them.

The completed Terrier.

CHAPTER FIVE

SOUTHERN REGION ARCHITECTURE

WHAT IS THE BEST APPROACH?

To establish how best to set the scene in a Southern Railway layout, the first thing to do is to look at a few basic principles. The Southern Railway, as it became in 1923, was made up of three main companies: the London, Brighton & South Coast Railway (LBSCR), the South Eastern and Chatham Railway (SECR) and the London and South Western Railway (LSWR), not forgetting the LSWR's working interest in the Somerset and Dorset Line. That much is fairly common knowledge. However, what is often conveniently forgotten is that these three, through various takeovers and amalgamations, were made up of over twenty independent railway companies (five alone on the Isle of Wight), stretching back in time to the London and Southampton Railway formed in

1834, which changed its name to the London and South Western Railway (LSWR) in 1838.

The underlying reason for the 1923 grouping was as a precursor to what was hoped would be full nationalization, due in part to the problems that the World War I government had had in dealing with dozens of railway companies in order to move supplies around the country. This compresses into a sentence what was in fact a highly complex set of pure business manoeuvres; if you wish to study these in more detail, there are many weighty books that explore the companies' histories. Interesting as it is, this does not directly concern us here. What it does illustrate is that the Southern Railway was not a comfortably formed and designed physical entity that had been planned a long way in advance. In reality it was a ragbag of widely different build-

Micheldever station. Originally built by the London and Southampton Railway and one of the oldest buildings on the BR(S) system. The building is now out of use to rail passengers.

ing styles of stations, signal-boxes and associated architecture designed by many different architects and engineers.

Thus there was not one purely Southern Railway style. What the Southern did do was to add its own designs into the mix with a set of quite stylish modern buildings – which of course only adds to the confusion of what is already a complex set of political and business ideas and ideals. The Southern Railway was there to achieve an administrative goal, not because it was necessarily the best way of doing the job on the ground. The internal politics existed long after its formation in that the LSWR had a controlling element that would influence many of the decisions taken throughout the life of the company and beyond.

The point of this preliminary discussion is to highlight that there is no all-encompassing approach possible for the modeller. If you are looking to model an exact prototype situation of, say, a particular station, then of course this line of questioning doesn't apply as the answers are already there in front of you – but this is an approach that few take, most preferring a little, or sometimes a lot of freelancing to take place. This is no bad thing, but to convince both the builder and any third party viewer, there are a couple of things you must decide: first, where you want your layout to sit geographically; and second, which of the parent companies are likely to have built/run your freelance line. When these have been decided, then you can construct/ buy your model architecture to reflect this.

It is often quite feasible for 'foreign' locomotives and rolling stock to appear in an area, as the photographic historical instances are often there to back this up. However, if you say you are building a model based in mid-Kent, and then place an LSWR stone-built signal-box on the layout, it will simply look wrong, and you can't expect any sort of visual credibility from anyone, including yourself. A South Eastern Railway Saxby and Farmer type timber or timber/brick box will sit much more comfortably on the scene. What is more, it will define the scene much more quickly than any rolling stock.

The small advantage in modelling the nationalized

British Railways (Southern) period is that not only can you include the pre-1923 grouping company buildings, of which many survive to this day, but you can also add many Southern Railway structures that may have upgraded the line. Furthermore you can then add any war-time or post-war British Railways buildings that may have been subsequently introduced. One of the joys (or problems) is that we are dealing with a fluid situation. You only have to look at the houses around you to realize that it doesn't take long for owners to extend and adapt their properties, and so it was with the railway.

The pre-grouping modeller is not so lucky in this regard, but the Southern Region modeller could, for instance, have an LBSCR station building with Southern replacement concrete platforms, and a 1940s ARP (air-raid precaution reinforced) signal cabin, and could run 1970s blue-grey 4CIG multiple units through the station. At first glance none of these logically go together, and yet similar prototype scenarios existed all over the system, almost up to the present time.

So with all this apparent contradiction of building styles, what constitutes and tells the viewer that it's a Southern Region station? In a simple phrase: 'The

---

TIP: STUDY POST-WAR RAILWAY PHOTOGRAPHS

Study any post-war railway photograph, date the scene, and then sub-date first the rolling stock and then any railway buildings. Write this down, and continue through several similar photographs until you can gauge the balance of building styles and build periods for an area. If the scene is urban, also look at the housing styles: are these Victorian terraces, 1930s semi-detached villas or 1960s high-rise blocks? What came first? Did the railway cut through, or – more likely – did the housing developers build around a line to gain sale value to commuters?

overwhelming presence of green paint.' What the viewer will see first is colour, followed by the building style. So as long as the colour does not suggest one of the other nationalized regions, the viewer will initially be fooled. It is then up to the modeller to introduce other key factors to the scene, as already discussed.

A final note before we delve into the building projects: if the scratch-building of structures is new to you, you may wish to start with the smaller auxiliary buildings in the next chapter. All are relevant to the Southern Region, but they may be less daunting a build for the novice, starting with an easy project: a concrete hut kit.

SIGNAL-BOXES: INDICATORS OF PLACE AND PERIOD

As intimated above, signal-boxes are often the strongest indicator of place and period. Many of the pre-group signal-boxes are still with us, but due to obvious technological advances are disappearing at an alarming rate. It's very easy to think that the pre-group boxes are the whole story, and where a line has remained on the original alignment and with the same safety requirements, the old boxes have survived. However, as the large area-wide power boxes have taken over, the earlier boxes are being demolished because they are no longer of use.

The Southern Railway built a number of large new boxes between the wars, often in the then ultra-modern Art Deco style. Several of these remain, for example at Dorking, Bognor and Deal. They are very stylish, but unless you are building a large station model, they are possibly too big. If you do require one, then a cast resin 'ready-to-plant' model is available from Bachmann in 4mm scale.

Portsmouth harbour signal-box. Built by the SR in the 'Art Deco' style.

Air-raid precaution signal-box at Gomshall. The station opened on 20 August 1849 for the Reading, Guildford & Reigate Railway, but this signal-box was constructed in 1941 to the Southern Railway's Type 14 air-raid precaution design.

At the opposite end of the style spectrum are the air-raid precaution (ARP) boxes, built to withstand any blast damage from Luftwaffe bombs. This solid build seems to be true, as the remaining ARP boxes have been notoriously hard to demolish. The styling is very stark and square, but a few are preserved – a Southern Railway example still stands at Gomshall station in Surrey. Post-war, the British Rail design team took over. Several pre-group boxes were replaced as line upgrades were implemented, often with a standard design box that could be adapted to fit the situation, from large town boxes to small single-storey cabins. A medium-size British Railways box remains in use at Lancing, built in 1965 to replace the small LBSCR crossing cabin.

For the Southern Region modeller who wants do something a little different, then one of these post-grouping designs will not only set the period but will move the layout away from the clichéd pre-group building. It is also ideal as a simple entry point for the novice who wants to construct his or her own buildings, but needs an easy project to start with in order to get to know the techniques.

BUILDING ALBANY PARK CABIN

Albany Park is a station built on the original South Eastern Railway's line between Dartford and Hither Green, and is a classic commuter-belt station. Albany Park was not originally planned on the line, but as housing spread out from London, the Southern Railway was quick to capitalize on this development and built numerous stations just for this growing and profitable traffic. The station layout itself is about as simple as you can get, with just a single platform on each side of the running lines, and no goods facilities. A signal-box was required, but with no pointwork it only needed to be modest.

There is some confusion as to the building date of the box, with either 1935 or 1948 given in listings. My guess is that as the station was opened in 1935, this date would seem to be the more logical, making it a pure Southern Railway design – if you can call it design. It is no more than a simple brick block house some 12 feet by 11 feet in plan, with a

concrete roof; it would hardly win any imagination awards. This does, however, make it perfect for our needs: a small Southern Railway or British Railways (Southern) box that is simple for the novice to construct from just two packs of Wills Scenic Series material and a little plastic sheet and strip, making it not only straightforward to build, but economical as well.

PROJECT SIX: A SIGNAL-BOX

Tools:
- Cutting mat
- Liquid solvent
- Needle files
- Sanding stick
- Paint
- Knife or scalpel
- Steel ruler
- Square
- Pin chuck and drill bits
- Saw

Materials:
- Wills building sheet SSMP226 brick
- Wills Scenic Series pack doors and windows SS86
- 20-thou plastic sheet
- 40-thou plastic sheet
- 40 × 40-thou and 10 × 20-thou plastic strip

CUTTING WILLS SHEET

The first task is to cut out the walls from two of the sheets in the pack. Cutting the sheet is tricky until you get used to it. The basic method is to mark your cut line in pencil, then using a knife and steel ruler, make two or three light cuts. Then gently bend the sheet so that the cut opens up, but does not break. Then finish off with more gentle passes with the knife. This gives a clean edge, while just bending and snapping will leave a ragged edge with usually some surface damage, especially on the brick sheet.

Cut a strip of sheet full length and 40mm high (which equates to thirty brick courses, if you prefer). Cut this into two equally sized lengths of

Rear wall with bricks 'scribed' on.

Doctored window frame on the left, the original on the right.

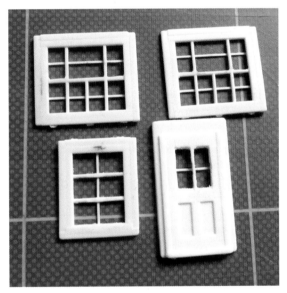

Completed windows and door.

48mm each, leaving a waste piece of around 45mm. Repeat this with a second sheet, only this time creating two matching 44mm lengths. As you do this, keep checking that all is square and that both pairs are all of the same 40mm/thirty course heights. You should now have two pairs of front/back and ends, which should be lightly cleaned up with a sanding stick.

Taking one of the 48mm pieces, scribe three lines at the upper rear at 1mm intervals with the knife blade held at an angle, and mark off dummy brick courses as shown. Then cut a 'drain' 4mm from the left-hand end and 4mm wide down to the bottom of these brick course lines. Repeat the scribing of dummy brick courses on the other three wall pieces, making sure that all courses correspond with the neighbouring wall both front and back.

WINDOWS

Take the large windows from the pack and 'thin' the bars very carefully with a needle file. Add extra bars by adding lengths of 10 × 20-thou strip to the rear of the frame as shown, then remove the upper central bar to leave two larger panes uppermost.

Add a single horizontal bar to a medium-sized window, as shown. Take one of the door mouldings and drill out the upper panels, leaving the vertical bar. Clean the holes with a needle file and thin the

central bar to match the 20-thou strip. Then add a horizontal bar as shown. Finally paint the door and window units Southern green.

Mark a window opening in the second long (48mm) wall, 16mm high by 18mm wide positioned 15mm from each end and 12mm top and bottom. This is done using the same chain-drill method used earlier on the Terrier locomotive (see p.60). Drill holes round the inside of the markings, join them using a knife, push the waste piece out, and sand back to the line using a sanding stick and needle files.

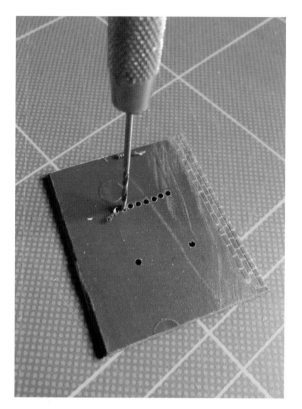

Window aperture being removed using a chain drilling technique.

Mark a line 1mm below the scribed brick courses and add a strip of scrap plastic below this line. This is to give the roof piece something to sit on. Cut a recess 18mm wide by two brick courses high at the central bottom using two saw cuts and the score,

End wall with added brickwork, mitred edges and floor support piece.

bend and cut method as before. This is the exit for the signal rodding. Then add the window unit and allow this section to harden off while adding similar roof support strips to the other walls in the same position.

MITRED EDGES

You will see that the edges have been mitred at 45 degrees. This is a straightforward process that requires a home-made tool: simply a scrap of sand-paper stuck completely flat to a scrap of chipboard or MDF. The wall is held at an angle very slightly less than 45 degrees, and rubbed back and forth until a sharp edge is created without losing any of the length on the outer face. It may be worth practising on a piece of scrap sheet first. This mitre technique will be used to construct all the buildings in this chapter.

Creating the mitre using a sanding board.

Add the other large window unit to the end wall using the same aperture size, about 12mm from each edge and again 12mm from the bottom edge. Mitre the edges as before.

Take the other end wall and cut a 12mm-wide doorway 4mm from the left-hand edge, 29mm high, using saw cuts on the vertical lines and a score method for the top edge. Cut a window opening 7mm from the right-hand edge 17mm high by 13mm wide, with the top edge level with the top of the doorway. Square both these apertures with a

Door wall with the door and window fitted.

Three walls assembled. Note the corner fillet.

needle file, then add the window and door units and mitre the edges.

At this point the walls can now start to be assembled, making sure that all is square, and possibly adding a small fillet of plastic behind each joint. When assembled, the outside face of the corners can be tidied up by running a triangular or half-round needle file around the corners at each mortar course – this gives the building a complete feel, rather than it looking like four separate pieces.

DETAILING THE WALLS

Cut a strip of 20-thou sheet 3mm wide, and cut it into lengths 4mm wider than each window and door

aperture, and also the rodding cut-out at the lower front, to represent the lintels. Add these strips at the top of each opening. Scribe a piece of scrap plastic to represent the vertical 'soldier row' of brick at the bottom of the doorway, and fit in the gap below the door.

A roof section from 40-thou sheet can now be cut to drop into the top. This should be about 45 × 41mm, but discrepancies in cutting or fitting may alter this size, so measure the opening before you cut. Trial fit this piece until you get a tight fit, and attach it making sure that it is level all round with the bottom of the internal brick line. Window sills can also be added from 40 × 40-thou strip, allowing 1mm extra length on each side. This strip can also be used to add the dummy roof edge by laying slightly over-long strips into the brickwork exactly level with the roof line, and trimming to length.

PAINTING

When all this work is hardened off, paint the inside of the cabin. Most public buildings of this type and period seem to be cream, duck-egg or pale blue, very much the same colour range as the underside of aircraft. I can't help thinking that this is more

Complete cabin less glazing.

than coincidence in post-war buildings. Give the brickwork a base colour of Humbrol 70, and paint all lintels, sills and the roof concrete colour. I tend to mix a pale grey and sand (Humbrol 45 and 64) to get something close. Concrete is a difficult colour to replicate, and some experimentation may be necessary. With a small brush, add dark grey to a few random bricks on each wall, and a similar amount touched in with dark orange (Humbrol 62). When dry, a careful wash of pale grey can be spread over the brickwork and allowed to settle in the mortar lines.

FINAL CONSIDERATIONS

At this point there are questions that can be asked. A drainpipe with a hopper at the top could be added at the rear, using either a Wills moulding, or simply a square piece of plastic and a length of 40 × 40-thou

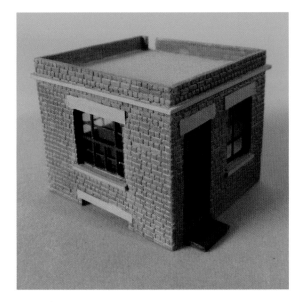

Completed cabin.

Typical Kentish box at Sheperdswell.

TIP: USE CARDBOARD AND BRICK PAPER

If you are nervous about using Wills building sheet, then this cabin can be built with cardboard and brick paper; 2mm artist's mounting card would be best. The walls would need the length measurement of one pair to be reduced by the thickness of the card, and the walls made up as a long strip with the apertures cut out. The corners would need to be scored inside to allow the structure to be folded. The outside would be covered in brick paper with enough excess at the top edge to fold over the top three courses. The paper over the windows should be pierced in the centre, and diagonal cuts made to the corners and the four flaps folded back. The Wills windows would still be the simplest method. The door, lintels and roof could all be made from card.

strip. In period photos there appears to be a stove-pipe chimney at the rear of the cabin. Similar boxes did have stoves, and some were built with a small brick chimney stack at the rear. A suitable pipe could quickly be made from a length of redundant biro refill painted very dark grey. These details to the rear of the cabin depend very much where it will be sited on the layout: if the rear is hidden, there seems little point in going to the extra trouble.

The other question is the interior. This particular cabin is not too bad as the windows are quite small; larger signal buildings have a great deal of glass and do need detailing inside. According to published signal diagrams (available on line), the Albany Park cabin had only four levers inside. You could buy one of the excellent interior detailing packs, but a small floor block and angled pieces of 10 × 20-thou strip suitably painted would give enough visual information to fool the viewer into thinking that there was much more detail than there actually

is. These levers can be set on a floor section fitted in a similar way to the roof. Do note that it needs to be at least two brick courses up, and level with the foot of the door to allow for rod and crank runs underneath.

STATION BUILDINGS

If signal-boxes are very indicative of railway company area, then station buildings are the wild card. Certainly you do have to be slightly careful in placement, but generally it is the building material that is geographically specific; the designs are extremely

Preserved LSWR station at Corfe in Dorset.

wide-ranging even in the same area. These range from the basic, such as the Colonel Stephens designs for the Hawkhurst line and the Kent and East Sussex light railway line (which was finally taken into the national system in 1948 after escaping the 1920s grouping), with the accent on late Victorian corrugated iron structures, which were not too far from agricultural designs, to William Tite's LSWR classical columns at Gosport, and just about everything in between. They encompass the stone of the LSWR's West Country lines, the brick of Sussex and Surrey with their 'cottage' designs, the Art Deco and brutalist shapes of the Southern Railways' 1930s, to the Victorian Gothic such as at Etchingham, built this way to appease the local landowner. Once you move out of the capital and outside the larger termini, then really anything is possible, even on adjacent stations on the same line.

While signal-boxes are functional structures, and although visible, are not part of the public domain, the station building contains the ticket office, waiting rooms, refreshments and the like, and is very much the public face of the railway: built to impress, built to make a statement, built to inform the passenger that he is in safe hands. So even though there is actually no technical reason why the building should exist (the railway could run without it, unlike a signal-box), it's very obvious where the design and building money has been spent.

Of course the pre-group companies were to some extent in competition with each other, wooing the passenger to take their route to the destination, so the grander the design the better, sometimes even on tiny wayside stations. By the time the Southern Railway took over there was an element of a 'brave new world' at hand. The new push to electrify the

Brick-built LSWR station at Wareham.

ABOVE: **Italianate styling at Portslade waiting rooms. Several of the ex-LBSCR stations on the coastway line were built in similar style.**

Pure Southern Railway design at Tolworth. Almost everything is constructed from concrete.

ABOVE: **Not all SR 1930s buildings were Art Deco stylized. This is 'no frills' brick brutalism at Albany Park station. Although hardly beautiful, this is a classic building and perfect for a post-war urban model.**

LEFT: **More simplicity at Bishopstone. Built in 1938 as part station, part pillbox, the building is still complete with gun slits in the upper storey. The Art Deco concrete buildings may represent the age of Southern Electric trains, but this and Albany Park give more of a workaday feel.**

entire system meant that new buildings on new stations would reflect this modernity, and sweeping shapes in gleaming concrete were the order of the day, quickly referred to as 'the Odeon style' after the similar contemporary moving picture houses. Although the Odeon stations were not the only features that the Southern Railway built, in pure hardware terms they are to some extent the SR's legacy. Most of the company's rolling stock production is long gone, or tucked away on preserved lines, but the concrete stations still remain today for thousands of passengers on their daily commute.

By the mid-1930s things were a little more austere, and building styles reflected this. There was less need to show off, and it was clear that commuters to the capital were a different breed to the travellers of earlier times, and a more basic set of facilities could be installed. The Albany Park signal cabin illustrated in the foregoing project is a product of this period, as is its accompanying station building pictured on page 78. There's quite a jump in thinking from the photo of Tolworth's design to that of later infill stations such as Albany Park. These are the extremes, however, and there are a few designs that find middle ground between the two.

WHAT TO MODEL

As was discussed in the opening chapter, you first need to have some idea of where you want your layout to be set, and then base everything else around that decision. I did indicate that many of the modelling projects would be linked to the Central Section as they have to be set somewhere. So assuming you are building a station – and remember, doing this is not compulsory – and you have decided on an area, you need to ask the following questions: first, which company built it and when? Second, what material did they use? And third, why was it built?

Why it was built is not such a foolish query as it appears, as railway companies built stations for specific reasons and traffic flows, and not on a whim (see Albany Park, opposite), and this would affect the size and perhaps the style. Thus it is doubtful

that Gosport would have been built to such a grand design if Clarence Yard had not been the waving-off point for the royal crossing to the Isle of Wight and Queen Victoria's Osborne House, while Newhaven Town, which is effectively in the same position, being the last stop before the passenger terminal en route to Dieppe, is little more than a wooden shed. All these factors will determine what your station building looks like and how big it is, coupled with how much space you have at your disposal.

Finally it would be a mistake to think that country station equals small buildings and town station equals big: they don't. Rural land was cheap and the expectations may well have been high, so country stations are often large and sprawling, built with the air of expectancy of traffic that in fact never came. Conversely the late period urban station was usually shoe-horned into expensive land and was often very cramped for the passenger. Anyone who has experienced London's Underground at rush periods will attest to this. Again, don't assume: observe and replicate.

A LONDON, BRIGHTON AND SOUTH COAST RAILWAY 'COTTAGE'

The London, Brighton and South Coast Railway took in most of Sussex, with its large clay deposits, so the natural building materials are brick and tile. This is reflected in many of the older properties in the area. The Lewes and East Grinstead line, opened in 1882, featured a style that came to be known as 'cottage' because of its similarity to the building style of many local rural houses, with a brick lower floor and hung tile-clad upper floors. Stations such as Sheffield Park, Chailey and Newick and Horsted Keynes (locally pronounced 'Canes') all feature this style, and luckily have been partly preserved. The 4mm modeller is also in luck as the hung tile pattern has been produced in the Wills building sheet range. Not only that, but one of the Wills Craftsman Kits is designed to look very much like one of these classic Sussex stations. This, then, is the subject of the next project.

ABOVE: **LBSCR 'cottage' station at Horsted Keynes.**

Horsted Keynes side elevation. In some ways this is the 'perfect ideal' for most branch-line modellers – pretty and ornate.

TIP: ALWAYS TAKE A CAMERA WITH YOU

Always take a camera with you and photograph suitable buildings from several angles. If the building is not built from an easily calculated material such as brick, try to get at least one shot containing a person of known height; then at least you have some reference point with which to measure the size of the structure. You can also assume that a standard single door is about 2ft 6in (80cm) wide and 6ft 6in (2m) high.

Horsted Keynes was a junction. Traffic could run from Lewes, and all points south, to East Grinstead and on to London via Oxted. Alternatively it could cut through north-eastwards from Haywards Heath on the Brighton–London line, which provided a very useful secondary avoiding route – until in 1955 the Transport Committee (CTCC) decided

to close the line. However, local opposition found that the original act stated that four trains a day *must* run between certain stations on the line, and the CTCC withdrew its decision; subsequently it followed this ruling to the letter, running four trains to these stations only, but at times of the day when no one wanted to travel – it became known locally as the 'stroppy service'. Thus by deviously running trains at non customer-friendly times, after over a year the CTCC proved that the line could not operate at a profit, and it was eventually closed in 1958. Happily it reopened as the Bluebell Railway, and can be seen today in full preservation running from Sheffield Park to East Grinstead.

PROJECT SEVEN: THE WILLS CRAFTSMAN STATION KIT

Wills Kits produce a boxed kit, which, if not exactly like the LBSCR cottage station, certainly gives the flavour of it. If you wish to do no modelling at all, it is possible to buy the Bachmann resin ready-to-plant model of Sheffield Park station, but this book is primarily about making things, so we'll build on

The raw materials: Wills sheet and the templates. Mark each sheet 'top' and 'bottom' in pencil.

the skills used with the signal cabin and expand them slightly to construct something a lot bigger.

I have to say straightaway that the Craftsman kits are not strictly kits in the usual accepted form, and opening a box for the first time may be quite daunting. What you get is not a set of parts to put together, but enough basic materials for you to actually make the parts to put together, and a set of templates to help you. Essentially this is exactly the same idea as the signal cabin, but there is much more of it. So the first thing to do is sift through all the sheets and mouldings, check them against the templates, and sort them into containers such as ice-cream tubs, only keeping to hand those that are needed immediately.

It is also worth pointing out that you don't actually need to buy the kit, which is simply a bundle of sheet packs, and you could easily work out how much material you'll need and buy the individual packs. For example, you would need two packs of brick, one pack of plain tiles and one pack of fancy tiles for the main structure. You won't save very much over the whole project, but financially it would be an easier way in. What you won't get, of course, are the all-important templates.

THE WALLS

The project starts with the walls, and the templates are their 'front face', so if you are working on the back of the sheet as usual you have to think in reverse. First, mark top and bottom ('T' and 'B'), clean off the edge tags, and make a careful start in marking out the first sheet. The method of removing window apertures is the same as the signal cabin with a chain drill technique, and doorways are made by cutting the sides and scoring the top as

ABOVE: **Simple shapes can be cut out using a razor saw.**

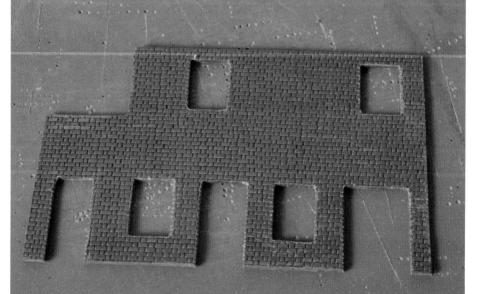

Front wall with all the openings removed.

before. The main parts can be removed by scoring and bending, or by sawing. For example, the first wall should look something like the photo opposite below. Some of the wall joints are mitre joints, as with the signal cabin, but there are a couple of square butt joints that only need cleaning up.

* **Remember:** If you are working on the back of the sheet, then you need to flip all the marking left for right. Check and double check before cutting as you progress, number each part as you go, and take your time.

There are a couple of arched soldier-row parts to add; these can be cut from the parts supplied. It's best to cut a piece slightly longer and then trim it to fit. There are also flat concrete keystone lintels included; these can be thinned down and added after the window frames have been put in.

FITTING THE WINDOWS

Once the window sills have been added from the strip provided, the window frames, sills and lintels should be painted, and each completed wall given a coat of brick red.

Glazing material can now be fitted with a tiny drop of all-purpose adhesive, and dummy curtains added behind using coloured paper taken from magazines.

On the ladies' waiting-room windows dummy net curtain material can be added using strips of kitchen greaseproof paper, either over the whole window or, as here, just the lower half. This contrasts nicely with the other plain windows, and gives a human touch and a sense of purpose, and an outward indication of the room's use.

ABOVE: **Brick lintels are cut from the curved strips.**

Front wall with windows and doors added.

Window sills made from the strip provided.

'Curtain material' can be cut from magazine advertisements.

Glazing installed and 'curtains' added behind. This gives a 'lived in', human feel and softens the building.

Net curtains can be added using kitchen greaseproof paper.

Using a small engineer's square ensures that the walls will be built square and true.

ASSEMBLING THE LOWER WALLS

Once the lower walls have been completed, they can be assembled using a square to aid accuracy. The kit includes triangular 'fillet' pieces, which should be glued behind each corner. There is a possibility that even though you have built the corner square, the solvent will pull the walls inwards. So it's worth checking on the join a couple of minutes afterwards, and if necessary, adjusting the parts back to square before the joint cures.

THE GABLE ENDS

As can be seen from the prototype photographs, the gable ends feature an ornate framed rectangular window. The kit, however, includes arch-top frames – but these are quite easy to alter. Add lengths of 40 × 40-thou plastic strip to both top and bottom of the rectangle, and then edge the sides with the same strip to create a deeper frame. Then, and only then, cut off the arch top section and clean up. This means you must ignore the templates for the gable ends, and cut the aperture using these new frames as a guide.

When the upper floor walls have been added, fit a dummy floor from plastic or card, and when this is set, add vertical blanking walls. Unless you want to add a fully detailed interior, these just need to stop the light bouncing around so the viewer is

Lengths of 40-thou square strip are stuck on to create a new, deeper frame.

Crude internal walls from thick card are painted black to stop light reflection and prevent the viewer looking right through the building.

prevented from seeing straight though one window and out the other side, so they can be quite crude pieces of card. When fixed, paint them black.

THE ROOFS

The roofs are probably the trickiest part. Start by adding the long gable first, as this is the most straightforward shown here on the right. Then trace the templates for the left hand on to another fairly stiff piece of paper, cut them out and trial fit. Because of probable errors in the cutting and building so far, there will probably be a discrepancy in what the templates say and what actually fits, and the paper template will show where any problems

Roof sections now fitted. Allow an extra course of tiles top and bottom when cutting to give room for adjustment.

occur. This way you can draw as many paper roofs as you need until you are happy with the fit. This saves wasting the plastic sheet by possibly cutting a part that is wrong, and which will need to be discarded. The roof section measurements are very tight, working to the outside limit of the Wills sheet size, so this paper template procedure is time well spent.

CONSTRUCTING THE CHIMNEYS

Chimneys can be constructed in two ways: either cut them as four separate pieces of equal height and assemble them using a mitre joint as you did for the walls; or score the sections and open up the cut into a V-shaped groove and fold as shown in the illustration. Either technique will work equally well, but the latter is less fiddly and will generally result in a squarer assembly. Capping can be added from scrap 40-thou sheet and given a slight chamfer.

Pots should ideally be added at the very end of the build, as handling will often cause them to get knocked off. Remember to vary them a little in size, and if possible replace them with cast white-metal or scratch-built examples. A quick look upwards to any chimney stack of any age will demonstrate how different pots are grouped on the same stack due to damage and replacement over the years.

At this point the stack can be bedded in with a little plastic filler or even UHU, shaped with a cocktail stick or similar. It is unlikely they will be a perfect fit in the roof openings, and this suggestion of lead-work flashing around the base will hide a multitude of sins.

GUTTERS AND DOWNPIPES

Gutters and downpipes can now be added from the component sprues, noting that there are two different size pipes: the larger for the main roof gullies, and the smaller for the area around the gents toilet. The guttering can be added as supplied, but benefits from being 'hollowed out', first by running a knife along the centre line, then gently filing the U shape with a rat-tail needle file.

ABOVE: **Chimney stacks can be 'folded' by filing a deep 'V'.**

RIGHT: **Reinforcement bands fitted, and a top from 40-thou sheet. Its edges are rounded with a sanding stick to represent the cement bed.**

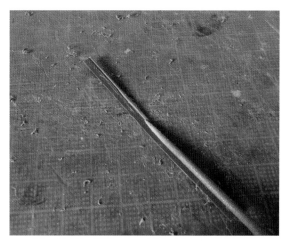

A gutter strip is opened up using a round or oval needle file.

SUMMARY

This project will give you a station building that will look at home on any part of the central section of the Southern Region. The same design in stone sheet might just work for a Western section building, but the Eastern section structures are of a completely different type and rely quite heavily on timber cladding, so a little research and planning would be needed.

As it stands the structure is rather plain, and further detailing can be added such as timetable notice boards and enamel advertising boards. However, in this state it could also be used as a Sussex-style house at the line side, with the addition of suitable details such as a garden and washing line,

The basic completed structure.

or as the basis for a farm scene with the addition of open-fronted barn buildings. The kit is only a base and can be built in many different ways to suit the situation.

GOODS SHEDS

The Southern Railway goods shed is not a prominent construction, and like anything else to do with

RIGHT: **Large LBSCR goods shed at Arundel station. Not unusually the surviving buildings have been turned over to industrial use – here a builder's merchant.**

BELOW: **The attractive preserved goods shed at Corfe, with the less attractive block-built lean-to. These later additions are a must for the BR(S) modeller, as most pre-group stations had been altered in some way by the post-war period; block, asbestos and corrugated iron sheet were the materials of choice in many cases. These simple additions can lift a building from the 'historically twee' to something more seriously realistic.**

Southern freight handling, it tends to hide away from the camera. Like the wagons it served, its existence was mostly ignored. Part of the problem once again is that of numbers. As modellers we tend to think (or have been conditioned to think by the model media) that every station site has a goods shed placed at the end of a siding or behind the platform of every single town in the land. This, of course, is far from accurate, and particularly so in the case of our subject area, with only larger stations being furnished with the traditional square brick over-shed or warehouse – and even then only where the traffic was deemed sufficient to warrant building one.

The result was that you could travel a considerable distance, and pass several stations, before any serious freight-handling facilities came into view. Today research is tricky, as many of those that were built have been swept away to make room for car parks and the almost compulsory supermarket, which developers delight in building on ex-railway land. However, for the determined there are one or two left to see.

BRICK SHED AT COOKSBRIDGE

The subject for the next project is a small brick shed situated at Cooksbridge in Sussex. Taking into account the reasoning above, it seems a very small stopping place for a goods shed – even now trains only stop during peak periods. The suggestion is that as the area is surrounded by farms, the shed was built to handle the large demand for inward and outward traffic from local agriculture. The station at 'Cook's Bridge' (the original spelling) was built by the LBSCR in 1851.

The shed was constructed by one Robert Bushby for the railway company for the sum of £285 sometime after 1854, suggesting that there was a clamour

Cooksbridge goods shed, built for the LBSCR in the nineteenth century. It is still intact, but has been altered internally; the changes to the door are shown. The shed is now on private land owned by a builder's merchant.

for freight facilities soon after the station had been opened. The shed was officially closed in 1977, leased to the adjacent wood yard, and sold to them in 1984. So although it is very visible, it stands strictly on private land. The building has been considerably altered over the interim period, so there is quite a large measure of conjecture involved with modelling it, especially with regard to the interior. There is a similar building at Angmering on the coastway line, which, as part of a retail unit, is slightly more accessible.

PROJECT EIGHT: SCRATCH-BUILT GOODS SHED

Materials:
The tools list is the same as the previous two projects, but as this is a scratch-build project there is a materials list as follows:

- 1 × Wills materials pack SSMP227 English Bond brick
- 1 × Wills materials pack SSMP203 slates
- 1 × Wills materials pack SS71 round-topped windows
- 1 × Wills materials pack SS46 building pack A
- Thin brick sheet (Wills flexible or Slaters)
- Clear plastic glazing material
- 60-thou plastic sheet (or scrap Wills sheet from the previous project)
- 30-thou plastic sheet
- 20-thou sheet
- 20 × 10-thou strip
- 40 × 20-thou strip

You may have some of this in stock already, so read the text carefully before buying the list.

The following project should give you a final model based on Cooksbridge goods shed, which is historically and dimensionally close, but not 100 per cent accurate. Note that the original is laid in Flemish Bond brickwork, whereas the plastic sheet is English Bond: this is so the 'round-topped windows' pack can be employed. The reason for using this pack is partly economic – the pack is 60 per cent

TIP: COLLECT PHOTOGRAPHIC EVIDENCE OF SUITABLE BUILDINGS

Routinely collect photographic evidence of suitable buildings for your area, and create excuses (without actually trespassing) to get close enough to record details. More importantly, don't keep this information to yourself, but please share it with like-minded people via the internet. Collecting the information is as good as useless if it is not shared with other people who are studying the subject.

more in cost – but aside from the windows, which will be adapted for the roof light, there are four brick sheets included as well. These have a strange cut-out and recesses designed to take the windows. Ignore this, as we only need the edges as shown below. There seems no point using a full-price pack if you are going to discard half the material. The full sheets are for the end walls, and the recessed sheets for the side walls.

CONSTRUCTING THE WALLS

Take one sheet of plain walling and cut a three-brick-course strip from the top. Then cut a section 70mm high by 115mm wide. The pilasters should be marked out at 9mm wide all the way round, which should give you a doorway of 43mm wide and an inset section of 42mm wide and 50mm high, set 10mm from the foot. The door height should be increased by 2mm to 62mm. Mark all this out, and check your measurements before you cut each piece.

Repeat this section with the other end, making sure that you make the cut-outs in mirror image compared to the first; this is obvious, but a very easy mistake to make.

The side walls are made from the recessed sheet. To make maximum use of this, study the

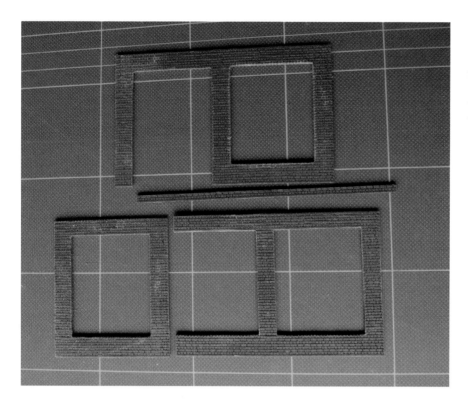

One set of walls cut out, the end wall above, and the two part side walls below. The three-course strip is for the gable-end roof line.

image above and note that the holes are cut so that there is a join at the thinnest part, thus reducing the cutting. So two parts are needed for each side: one 104mm long and one 61mm long, and both 70mm high to match the ends. The pilaster sections are again 9mm wide, giving a measurement run in millimetres of 9, 43, 9, 43, 9, 43, 9 (165mm in total). Note the side-wall insets are 1mm wider than in the ends. The side insets are 51mm high (43 × 51), giving a bottom-to-top measurement run of 10, 51, 9mm. Butt join these two sections together preferably against a straight-edge, but you may find it easier to sand the mitred extreme edges before you do this.

Repeat with the other side, but in addition cut the left-hand inset open down to the bottom for the doorway.

Cut seven brick sections 50mm wide and 60mm high to set behind the cut-outs. Before these are added, 'notch' all the mortar courses all the way round each cut-out on the main part with a triangular or oval needle file. Add the fill-in parts, and if not done beforehand, mitre all the edges.

THE GABLE END

Cut two triangular pieces for the gable end 24mm high and 115mm wide. Note that the slope runs to a point three brick courses from the bottom, not to the corner, leaving a square edge three courses

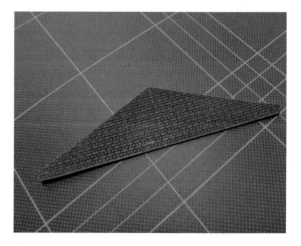

The gable end. Note the small notches at each end, allowing the piece to drop over the side walls.

Basic end wall with the extra roof-line piece to add.

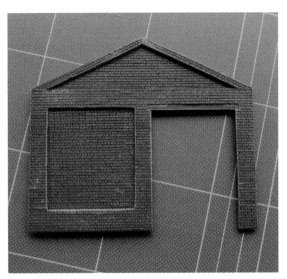

Wall complete with the doorway lintel cut in.

deep. These can now be filed back 2mm each side, and mitred to the inside. These three courses are an overlap that drops behind the end wall, so the cut-in at the ends allows for the top of the sides. Add the two triangles to the rear of the ends, with the bottom three courses hidden behind.

Take the first three-course strips cut at the very beginning, and add these to the top edges of the gables. Cut the angle at the top first, and then adjust the bottoms until they are a snug fit against the top of the wall. Then cut into the top of the doorway with a file by 3mm each side, and add a 3mm strip (reversed brick sheet) to represent the cast-iron

lintel. Repeat this with the other end and the side doorway.

THE DOOR RAIL

Next, to make the door rail, draw out the shape on 20-thou sheet. The rail should be 113mm overall in length and 3mm deep. Use a former or compasses to get the curves equal (I used an old till roll of about 18mm diameter). For the support girders, cut four short lengths of 40 × 40-thou strip and run a flat needle file down either side to simulate an I-girder. The length is not important as it can be sanded back later. Add these as shown, cut the rail from

Door side complete with the door rail fitted.

the sheet and add on top of the girders. Note the top of the rail sits four courses down from the top of the doorway, leaving the top open. It is in essence a gate more than a door. When the joints are hard, sand the I-girders flush with the rail.

THE DOOR AND DOORWAY

The door can now be cut from 30-thou sheet, 64mm wide and 52mm deep; the two end doors could also be made now, 46mm wide and 58mm deep. Scribe horizontal lines top and bottom 3mm up or down, then mark off 2mm intervals across the door and scribe the vertical planks from these marks. Add a foot brace along the lower horizontal line from 40 × 20-thou strip, and also add three roller plates from the same strip centrally and at 1mm from the edges. The rollers themselves can be made from 2mm rod slices, or by using a small leather punch. However, they are so tiny that it may be as easy to cut squares from the same strip, fix them on and then round them off with a needle file. Finally the crawl door framing can be added using 20 × 10 strip.

At this point the five doorway brick reveals can be made (9mm wide × 59mm tall) and fitted at the side

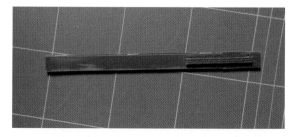

Internal platform face showing the reinforcing strip from scrap.

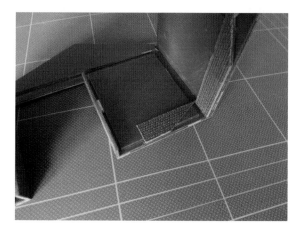

End and side showing scrap supports for the platform and the reveals at the doorways.

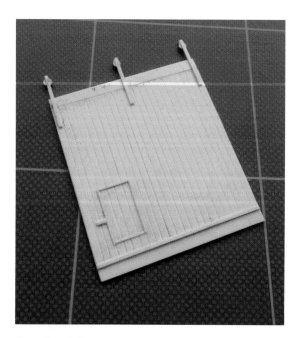

Completed door.

of each doorway edge. The possible sixth is optional as it is largely hidden behind the side door you have just made. All walls can now be put together.

Make up a platform facing strip 162mm long and 11mm deep, plus a similar piece 47mm long for the side door. Then add lengths of scrap 11mm deep around the bottom of the inside walls, fit the front facing behind the door reveals, and top with a platform.

FITTING THE PLATFORM AND SLIDING DOORS

The platform can either be scribed plastic sheet or, as here, Wills planking left over from the station building project. It should be around 56 × 156mm in size. An optional touch is to line the inside walls with some sort of brickwork. Here I used Wills flexible brick sheet, but Slaters brick sheet would

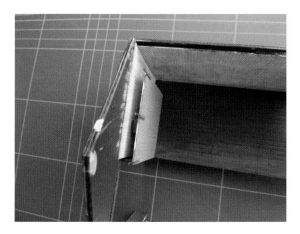

Platform fitted, along with the 'dummy' door.

work equally as well. The inside walls of goods sheds were often whitewashed for cleanliness and to reflect light; this was usually poorly maintained, however, and can be replicated with a very sloppy coat of white paint and washed over with dark grey.

The two sliding doors can be finished and painted. These would cut in at each end of the platform, but a little subterfuge can be employed and they can sit on top of the platform. Likewise the rollers and rail can be omitted, because although the door will be missed if it's not there, the tops disappear into the gloom of the roof.

FITTING THE WINDOWS

Take three of the window units and slice off the round tops as shown. Remove the outer edge of two of the units so that the outside frame of one becomes the new vertical bar for the next one. Butt-join the three together lengthways.

Frame the resulting large window with 40 × 40-thou strip, cut away the horizontal bars and clean up, then repeat with the other three window units. Paint both frames dirty white or cream, and put to one side.

FITTING THE ROOF SECTIONS

The two roof sections need to be exactly the same length as the shed. If all has gone well this should be 165mm, with a depth of 67mm. This necessitates a join, which can be problematic as the slate courses are not constant across the sheet. The best thing to do is to line this up with the roof-light opening to minimize the join. Cut one section 119mm long × 67mm deep, and a second 46 × 67mm deep. From the larger section remove a section 71mm long × 26mm deep from the top right-hand corner – join the remaining part and the short section, and add a reinforcement piece underneath from scrap. This should give you a broad U shape with a 71mm gap dead centre.

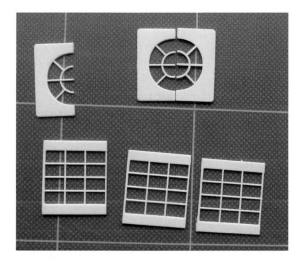

The three parts of one roof-light, with the lower and curved waste pieces above.

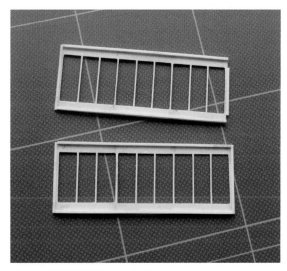

Complete roof-light sections.

Finally add a thin piece, two slate courses deep at the top of this space, creating the roof-light opening; this should end up 71 × 22mm. Repeat with the other roof section, and add the window units with the strip framing to the outside. This should bridge the roof joins and add a little more strength.

The roof pieces need to be almost flush to the gable-end top, so need to be thinned down.

Carefully file a step about 6mm wide at both outside edges. Then carefully again file a mitre on both parts at the ridge.

With the aid of some Blu-tack or plasticine to hold the roof sections to the shed, line them up and tack-join at the ridge. When you are happy with the fit – and this may take a little time to get right – firm up the join and add some scrap plastic underneath to support it. Finish painting the roof, add some clear plastic glazing to the inside of the roof lights, and fix the roof in place.

Cut a length of 20-thou sheet a little longer than the ridge and 8mm wide, lightly scribe the vertical slate joints, gently score down the middle and bend into a V. Paint, attach to the ridge, and trim as necessary.

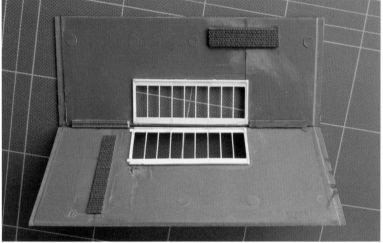

Complete roof showing scrap reinforcements. Note the thinning of the outside edges so the roof fits snugly over the gable walls.

FINISHING OFF

Finally paint the walls in the same manner as the first two buildings, add the gutters and downpipes from the buildings pack, and fix the side door with a little piece of packing at the bottom to support it.

This is not a 100 per cent accurate model of Cooksbridge shed as not only has it been altered somewhat over the years, but it is also hard to access and the main measurements were ascertained from photos. It does, though, capture the general feel of the building, representing a classic small Brighton shed.

The completed shed.

OTHER COMPANIES' SHEDS

Using all the above techniques it would be possible to build any similar set of buildings from the South Eastern & Chatham or London and South Western sections of the Southern Region, by simply observing and obtaining details in real life or from period photos, then adjusting the sheet material used, for example stone or clapboarding instead of brick. As was pointed out in the opening chapter, it is these local variations that really help establish the feeling of place, and in some ways generate the feel of the layout more than the rolling stock, especially in post-nationalized days, by which time the network had introduced more generic-looking rolling equipment.

TIP: USE WILLS STONE SHEET FOR LSWR BUILDINGS

For LSWR buildings Wills stone sheet is perfect, and a building could be made using exactly the same measurements above to give an ex-LSWR building; it would only need to be different in detail.

Rear of the LSWR Corfe shed, showing the canopy over the track side rather than the overall roof used in the demonstration LBSCR model.

CHAPTER SIX

ANCILLARY ITEMS

SOUTHERN CONCRETE BUILDINGS

Concrete used as a building material has been around since ancient times, so its use in the early twentieth century was hardly groundbreaking; nevertheless the Southern Railway quickly grasped its clean, modern look and took the architectural styling of the late 1920s and early 1930s period, namely Art Deco, and particularly its curved shapes, and used concrete to do this. Alongside its new futuristic stations the Southern Railway also took advantage of concrete's other useful property, and pre-cast many

parts not only for the stations but for many other small buildings and ancillary items.

Once again this was not a brand new idea: the Southern Railway was merely expanding the process set up by the LSWR at its plant at Exmouth Junction. Soon almost everything except the rails themselves could be turned out from this site, including platform faces and supports, fencing, lamp-posts, and particularly and famously its ready-to-install lineside buildings. This wholesale push for concrete soon gave the Southern Railway a defining look, which not only emphasized the modernity of the parts of the system that ran a slick modern electric pas-

1980s shot of a collection of concrete tool huts and platelayers' huts. Note the roof cut-outs and the outside taps, also the 'semi-detached' arrangement of three huts. This type of arrangement shows how to construct a natural, realistic scene, rather than just placing huts randomly at the lineside without a thought as to why they are there.

senger service, but was used to great effect by the company's advertising department.

By the time British Railways took over in the late 1940s, the system and look was so defined that there was no need to change to a more modern practice, and the concrete castings continued to be produced.

THE PLATELAYERS' HUT

Aside from the major structural station parts, the Southern designed a series of lineside buildings that could be easily transported on standard wagons to any part of the system, and could replace any of the more traditional (and locally built) structures that had traditionally been mostly built of timber. The most famous and recognizable (some would say iconic) is the angled roofed platelayers' hut. Out of all the lineside huts across the world, this is the one that tells you exactly where is should sit and where it came from. It is a pure Southern Railway building – except it isn't. The Southern did build concrete huts before the war, but the classic angled roof design is very much a post-war item: the first wasn't cast until 1946, right at the tail end of the Southern Railway era, then still technically in government hands post-war.

Production of the huts carried on through the 1950s and 1960s until the local track repair gangs were withdrawn, and lineside storage and shelter became redundant. The trap for the modeller of the classic 1930s Southern Railway is that these don't belong on a pre-war layout at all: they are very much a Southern Region item.

The notable shape of the huts was, of course, due to the transportation method. The point of the design was to do away with locally on-site constructed huts that needed constant repair, and replace them with an easily transported, pre-formed building that could be lifted on and off a standard-size flat wagon, and then later possibly moved somewhere else if required. Therefore the building itself had to be shaped to fit within the height of the smallest Southern Region loading gauge, hence the angled roof section. The chimney

---

TIP: LOOK OUT FOR STILL EXTANT CONCRETE HUTS

Most preserved Southern lines have a few standard concrete huts tucked away in odd corners; make a point of looking away from the more glamorous aspects of the line, and photograph them. Also look for still extant concrete huts in the lineside. Most of these are in quite a state, but they do show how the design could be customized to fit the desires of the local workforce.

---

was a separate item that was transported inside the hut and dropped on to the roof at the final site.

The huts were carried either on dedicated four-wheel flat wagons that were converted from ex-LMS and LNER mineral wagons (these carried one single hut), or on ex-Southern Railway 15-ton ballast wagons: these were long enough to carry the platelayers' hut and a matching concrete tool hut as a pair. The huts were fixed using a pair of three-part metal straps that ran up from each end and over the roofs.

The huts were distributed all over the region and sometimes beyond, but even though the railway saw the design as a great success, they were not universally liked by track gangs due to heat and condensation issues.

PROJECT NINE: KIT-BUILT BRITISH RAILWAYS (SOUTHERN) PLATELAYERS' HUT

There are currently two options for a 4mm-scale hut in kit form: the older is the white-metal product from Roxey Mouldings, the newer from Ratio Models in plastic. The latter is more easily available, but the former is slightly more accurate. For this section I used the Ratio kit, which comes in a pack containing two huts.

Tools: As for the previous building projects.

Materials:
• Ratio Models kit ref: 518
• Scrap plastic sheet, probably 20-thou
• Paint

For the more pedantic modeller there is a slight issue with this kit. Since its release it has been pointed out that it is slightly narrow. This is caused by the ends being 1mm undersized. When built up and on the layout this is not really noticeable, but it does affect the way the roof part sits. The remedy, if you wish to bother, is to slice out the central section of the ends and replace it with a wider piece of plastic sheet. However, during this build I decided to leave the ends as they were and to concentrate on a couple of modifications that lift the kit out of the ordinary.

The chimney parts should be painted black before assembly.

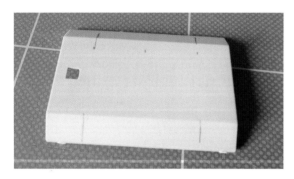

Hut roof with cut-outs marked in pencil.

THE LIFTING EYE AREA

The huts were delivered by hoisting (usually by rail-mounted crane) via four lifting eyes in the roof (there is a photo showing this particular action in *Branchlines to Horsham*, published by Middleton Press). After delivery the eyes were removed and replaced by ordinary bolts, which sat in recesses on the angled part of the roof. These were often, but not always, cemented over, creating a flush surface. The photo at the beginning of this chapter shows a pair that has been left.

To represent the lifting eye area, first clean up the roof part and mark the four recess points 9mm from each end and 2mm up from the edge. Drill into the top surface (but not right through) with a 1mm drill, then open up further with 1.5mm and 2mm drills. Square these drill marks using a knife with a new sharp blade to make flat, square recesses. Then add the chimney base, painting the inside of this black, and add the cap section on top.

FASHIONING THE WINDOWS

When transporting the huts by wagon the windows were plated over for protection; this was usually removed on arrival. However, later, due to vandalism and security, the windows were occasionally re-covered with plywood or steel, or had mesh added on the interior. To give a different feel to the straight-out-of-the-box kit, this can easily be replicated by adding a section of thin plastic sheet or card of about 20-thou thickness. The spare window mouldings can be put to one side for use in another project. All this can be done with the parts still on the sprue, as can the painting of the doors and any uncovered window frames in either green or dirty black.

FINAL ASSEMBLY

The rest of the kit can then be put together following the instructions, and painted concrete colour using a mix of pale grey (Humbrol 64) and sand (Humbrol 63) mixed equally. Concrete colour is tricky to replicate, but this mix gets fairly close. The window plating, if added, can be painted to represent either the original steel or wood, and the whole structure can be given a thin wash of German grey to represent weathering and to tone it down.

SOUTHERN REGION CONCRETE TOOL HUT

As stated above, the platelayers' hut was often paired with a square-based tool hut, which could be transported on the same vehicle.

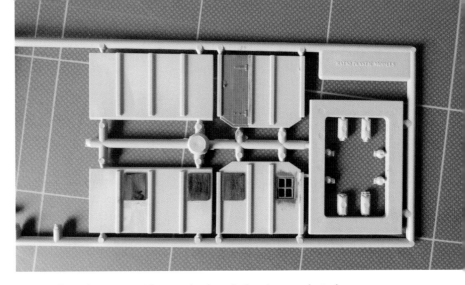

Parts still on the sprue with some basic painting done and windows detailed.

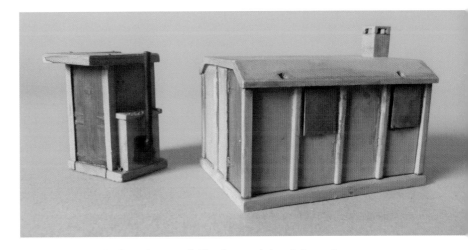

Platelayers' hut built and painted. The fogman's hut follows the same construction and is from a Roxey Mouldings white-metal kit.

Twenty-first century photo of a BR(S) hut showing the usual lineside condition with broken windows and 'tagging'. Finishing a hut in this condition would make an interesting small project for a late period layout.

PROJECT TEN: SOUTHERN REGION CONCRETE TOOL HUT

There is currently no 4mm kit available, so some easy scratch-building is required.

Materials:
- 60-thou plastic sheet or scrap Wills sheet from the previous building projects
- 20-thou sheet
- 40-thou sheet
- 20 × 40 and 10 × 20-thou strip
- Paint

For the base and roof: Cut three pieces of 60-thou, 27.5mm square. These form the base and roof. If you have built the goods shed or station from the previous chapter, you will probably have enough scrap brick sheet to use instead of new plain sheet. Just sand the brick face flat and use as new sheet, as was the case here. Two of these squares should be stuck together face to face, creating a 3mm-thick base (Wills sheet is 1.5mm thick, nominally equal to 60-thou).

For the walls: Cut a strip of 40-thou 26mm high by 96mm long, and slice off two pieces 25mm wide (the back and front walls) and two pieces 23mm wide (sides). Take one of the 25mm pieces and mark a central door 9mm wide. Scribe this with planks using a knife tip.

For the door surrounds: From the 20-thou sheet, cut a strip 2mm wide. Short strips are often better in this case as the thin material can flex slightly, causing the line to wander. Add one upright centrally on the back piece and two either side of the door on the front. Similarly add two central strips to the sides.

For the door: Add hinges to the door using two short lengths of 20 × 40 strip lightly sanded to a point at one end. Also add a latch on the door's opposite side. Add representations of hinges from 10 × 20-thou strip, and then stick the sides inside the ends, making sure that all is square.

For the corner pieces: Cut further strips of 20-thou sheet 4.5mm wide and score down the centre; it is easier if the scoring action is done first: mark, score, cut. Bend into 'L' shapes and add to the corners of the shed. You'll probably have a couple that will snap slightly along the score during this procedure: replace them, or run a touch of filler into the gap later.

Take the third square of 60-thou prepared earlier and add a piece of 40-thou, 26mm square on to the top with an even lip all the way around. Add tiny bolt heads from 10 × 20 strip in the corners.

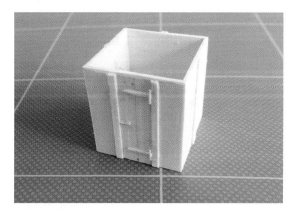

Basic walls of the tool hut constructed from plastic sheet and strip.

Corner pieces fitted. The lower roof and base made from scrap Wills sheet are also shown.

Finally: Add the three main parts together, making sure all is square and centrally located. Then paint as the platelayers' hut above with a concrete colour.

BUILD VARIATIONS

Both of the structures above went through several slight build variations: for instance, many tool huts had a sunken 'well' roof with a raised lip around the outside. The platelayers' hut roof profile changed over the years and various chimney pots of local character were added by the track gangs to improve drafting. A further representation of the second platelayers' hut in the pack would have been as a load strapped to a flat wagon. This could be achieved by taking almost any kit or ready-to-run wagon and converting it to a flat floor type, adding a hut in pristine condition, and making up the strapping using 1mm rod for the uprights and flat 40-thou strip for the horizontal sections that ran across the angled portion of the roof.

The Southern Railway and Region produced many other minor items in concrete, and many of these are easily modelled using similar techniques to the two items above.

Platelayers' and tool huts, along with a white-metal ballast bin from Roxey Mouldings.

Tool hut at Swanage.

SIGNALS

Modelling the signals of any British Railways region is not always straightforward, and the Southern is no exception. As with the buildings, there is a large spread of possible history to deal with, and annoyingly things are not always as neat and tidy as we may wish them to be. If you had told the 1960s-era railwayman that we would still be using Victorian-designed semaphore signalling in the twenty-first century, he would have laughed at you, such was the perceived pace of progress on the system at the time. However, that is certainly the case, and even stretches of main line in the area are, even at the time of writing, still controlled by semaphore arms. It would be unthinkable to our 1960s railwayman that the coastal services in 2016 are running up-to-date DMUs connecting with the high speed Eurostar service at Ashford, but still being signalled with semaphore arms on the main line west of Hastings.

TIP: KEEP LEFT-OVER PLASTIC SHEET AND STRIP

Keep a box of odd bits of left-over plastic sheet and strip to hand. Approximately 50 per cent of the tool hut above was made from scrap bits. A former margarine tub is ideal as a 'rummage' box.

A stunning display of semaphore arms at Hastings in 2015. Beyond this point semaphores are still predominant; behind the camera the signals change to colour lights (see the photo on page 12). There is a Class 170 DMU heading to Ashford in the distance. The line beyond Ore is still not electrified. Note the rarely modelled gradient road bridge.

In the introduction chapter I roughly split the British Railways (Southern) period into two: pre- and post-1968. In broad terms it's probably safe to say that if you are modelling the branch and secondary lines of the Southern Region in the 'pre'-period you will be fitting semaphore signals; the main line would be a mix of arms and various electrical displays. From the 1970s the arms started to disappear, while the branch and secondary lines had already largely gone – although as intimated above, this was a fairly long, drawn-out affair (colour light signals were introduced on the Southern Railway as early as the late 1920s).

Putting something as important as signals into a chapter entitled 'Ancillary Items' will enrage many readers, and I totally agree with them. However, the reality is that this is how many modellers regard them, and many do not even bother with them at all. This will be seen as madness by the student of the prototype, because without the signals there simply would be no railway. The misconception is that drivers (model or otherwise) drive the trains completely independently: they do not. They operate the train over a fixed route under the precise control of a set of instructions: signals.

After many decades of private car use we are conditioned to think that there is a degree of independence as a driver. The car allows us to divert around traffic signals or queues to suit ourselves. But the train driver has no such luxury and can only react to a set of commands – if a signal says stop, then that is what he definitely must do, and

there is no other option without the possibility of a calamity. In the case of a crash the very first thing to be examined is whether the driver ignored the signal, or did the signal fail.

Each individual line has its own signalling quirks, and each driver must undergo a period of route training before driving alone in order to understand any differences or oddities that that stretch of line may have. In model terms we should replicate this as far as is practical, and ideally signalling should be planned in from the start. On a typical model branch terminus this need not be too complicated.

Starter signal at Corfe. LSWR lattice style, but built by BR(S) in 1952.

If you are modelling a prototype, then the original signalling diagram can and should be obtained (these are available online or from books); this can then be used as a pattern from which to work, and if necessary adapted to the model's circumstance. On the other hand the freelancer should study similar diagrams from a series of different stations, and draw a conclusion as to what would be the most likely signalling arrangement for the layout.

Fitting your layout with signals lifts it visually. It creates a more serious feel, and it is often said that it is the addition of signals that is the difference between a model railway and a train set. The semaphore arm signal can be operated by a wire-in tube set-up – which is really just extending the linkage from the other end of the balance arm down through the baseboard, where it can be operated by hand via an 'L'-shaped crank. Alternatively a point motor can be used, again via a crank and with suitable 'stops' to drop the movement down to the small amount required.

Model signals for the 4mm Southern Region modeller are available in kit form in plastic, or for the more confident, as parts in brass. For the novice, the range produced by Ratio is possibly the best to start with. Three of these kits are specifically marked 'Southern Railway' (ref. 490/1/2/). However, as with the buildings, there is a wide historical base from which to draw. These three items are Southern Railway-designed upper quadrant (UQ) signals with plastic posts, representing those made from redundant rail. However, the reality is that, depending where you are in the region and how fast the replacement rate was, you also have the possibility of British Railways round post UQ signals, or any number of pre-grouping designs on square or lattice posts, which continued in use well into Southern Region days. This is certainly where the fun lies. Therefore don't take the packet markings as indisputable, but consider other options, and look carefully at the prototype that you wish to copy.

It would be impossible to outline every single signal option, so I'll take one specific semaphore to work on. The techniques can be adapted to deal with other similar semaphores.

THE HAYLING ISLAND ADVANCED STARTER SIGNAL

If you buy the Ratio Southern Railway signal kits mentioned above you will get a standard stop/distant signal, which is around 25 scale feet in height. This is all well and good if you want a post on an open line, but many signals are in fact designed to fit their surroundings, and vary from this. For example, a signal on the far side of a bridge may be taller so that it may be seen above the bridge parapet from a distance. Conversely a signal that only needs to be seen from quite close, such as a starter at the end of a platform, will be comparatively shorter than normal so that it is roughly at the driver's head height, or, as in the case of the example here, because it controls a low-speed shunting move where long-distance visibility is not required.

Advanced starters are set a distance from the platform end and generally repeat the information given by the platform starter signals, and/or are the final possible stop signal before the train leaves the station limits and enters the next section of line. The prototype example described was set at the limit of Hayling Island station and allowed shunting to take place up to, but not beyond it. This probably accounts for its relatively low height – it could be seen from up close without being way above the driver's head, and was clearly visible from the platform end as well. The signal and most of the station is long gone, having been swept away at closure in the 1960s; however, a very similar preserved example is shown below.

The Hayling Island signal was the original Saxby & Farmer item supplied at the line's opening (Saxby & Farmer were independent signalling manufacturers who supplied equipment to many pre-group railway companies). This signal lasted throughout the line's history, with a tapered wooden post and full length wooden arm. This is typical and prototypical, but a long way from what the kits marked 'Southern Railway' look like (all the Haying Island station signals were Saxby & Farmer up to closure, except one Southern Rail-built replacement in later years). Ratio do not produce a Southern Railway signal of this type, but this is where a little sideways thinking comes into play, as Ratio does produce a pack of LNWR (London & North Western Railway) signals with capped tapered posts, which are perfect for this project. In fact with a little light additional scratch-building you could build most of the Hayling Island station signals from this one pack.

PROJECT ELEVEN: HAYLING ISLAND ADVANCED STARTER SIGNAL

Tools:
- Pin chuck and 0.6mm drill
- Sanding stick
- Knife
- Needle files

Materials:
- Ratio LNWR signals Ref. 477
- 20 × 10-thou strip
- Scrap 40-thou sheet
- Scrap 20-thou sheet
- Micro-rod (optional)
- Peco track pins
- Paint

METHOD

The arms in the kit are a problem as they have a vertical corrugation. While still on the sprue, fill these with model filler (or Tipp-Ex), leave overnight, and then sand the arms flat. Next, give the arm and the upper glass lens two or three thin coats of red paint. Lastly finish off painting with the black/white stripes, lower lens and glass frame. Remember that the lower signal lens is actually blue and not green. All this painting is best done while the part is still on the sprue.

Drill through the hole in the arm with a 0.6mm drill to clear, then drill a new second hole approximately 2mm further to the left (this is to take the actuation rod). Cut the arm from the sprue and touch up any paintwork.

Working from several period photographs, I estimated the height of the post to be around 10ft, so look for the 53mm long post on the sprue and cut off the bottom of it, leaving the top three-quarters 40mm long. With the signal-arm barrel to the left of the post, sand the end of the barrel almost flush

Saxby & Farmer short-post signal at Sheffield Park: a wooden post and arm, but still in use well into BR(S) days.

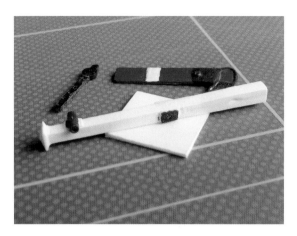

Hayling advanced starter signal components using LNWR parts: cut-down post with new lower pivot plates, filled and painted arm, a balance arm with new holes and a new plastic sheet base.

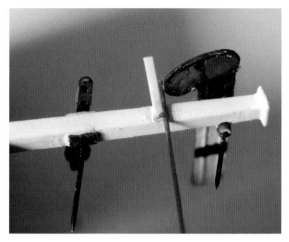

Close-up showing the fitting of the lower 'stop'. Watch those sharp points.

with the post, and run a drill through to clear the hole.

Add two tiny pieces of 20-thou sheet 2 × 3mm front and back at a position of 18mm from the foot of the post to represent the reinforcement plates. Drill through these from front to back with the same 0.6mm drill. This is the new pivot point for the balance arm, which should be tackled next.

Remove one of the balance arms from the sprue and gently sand the enlarged hole bumps flat. The 'inner' hole will become the new pivot hole, so drill two more holes 1mm apart towards the weight disc. The ground-plate bases in the kit are now not suitable, so cut a section of plastic sheet (40 or 30-thou thick) to about 15 × 13mm in size; paint it black at this point if you wish.

The next stage is really fiddly. Take a short length of micro-rod (½mm diameter was used here) and add it to the right side of the post sticking forwards, tight up under the cap of the post. Then add a second length 12mm further down the post. These act as 'stops' for the arm. Below this second rod add two pieces of 20 × 10-thou strip either side of the post. These are the ladder and step supports.

Take a Peco track pin (take care with these: they are designed to cut into baseboards and will do the same to your fingertips with relative ease) and

thread it through the signal arm and through the post barrel (with the barrel to the left). Then bend the pin very slightly downwards to retain it. Repeat this with the balance arm (using what is now the central of the five holes) and through the post with the weight to the left.

With both arms set in a matching horizontal plane, fit a length of wire supplied with the kit (approximately 28mm long in total) by turning each end over just past a right angle and slotting through the new hole in the signal and the far left hole in the balance arm. This is difficult to do with everything moving, so it is essential to clamp the foot of the post in a small vice or something similar so that both hands can be free.

Now you have a working signal you can add the peripheral items. A lamp can be cleaned up and fitted, as can the base with the post stuck to the rear of it, not centrally. A step from a 4mm square of 30-thou can be added to the step supports. Cut a section of ladder from the white sprue. Plastic ladders are notoriously fragile and the white one is a little tougher. If you are going to build a lot of signals, purchasing a few lengths of etched brass laddering is going to be less frustrating and visually a little finer, but of course is extra cost. Fit the ladder at a few degrees less than vertical and fix the top and bottom.

TIP: LOOK OUT FOR MODEL SIGNAL ENGINEERING PARTS

Keep an eye out at model railway exhibitions for the Model Signal Engineering range of signal parts. These are mostly produced in brass, and can be a useful to use with the Ratio range.

Finally add a length of wire from the top of the ladder to the top of the post over the top of the arm. This seems to have been common practice on some Saxby & Farmer signals rather than the usual body-hugging safety loops attached to a rear-mounted ladder. Any painting can now be completed.

Saxby & Farmer post in 1990 still in use as a fixed distant signal near Bishopstone. Note the more usual safety loop above the rear-fitted ladder, although the black mark above the arm may suggest that this was originally fitted with a handrail.

Complete Hayling advanced starter. Note the handrail and ladder position at the front.

THE LOADING GAUGE

An often ignored piece of railway equipment is the loading gauge. Each railway company had their particular design, but all had the same basic shape: a gallows-type post and a rail, which was usually curved, that hung below. The general idea was that it was far better for any wagon that was loaded too high to hit a swinging rail on the way out of a goods yard and be adjusted, rather than it demolishing the underside of a bridge a mile down the line. Incidentally the same system is still used on road construction sites to protect overhead power lines, and can often be seen at places where loaded dump trucks leave to rejoin the main carriageway. The rail could often be lifted to allow out-of-gauge vehicles to pass underneath.

The 4mm scale modeller has been well served with gauges over the years, and the most easily obtained is the Ratio Models gauge. This is Marked 'SR/BR', though this is hardly a common design for the Southern Region. A more accurate post for the more likely gauge would not be too difficult to scratch-build, or as below, you can use the post and rail from the Ratio kit and alter the lifting gear to represent the more common gauge.

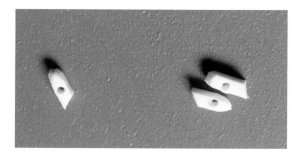

New 45-degree brackets to hold the top bar. The angled edge should attach to the top of the horizontal post.

PROJECT TWELVE: A LOADING GAUGE POST

Tools:

- Wire cutters
- Blu-tack
- Pin chuck and 0.5/0.6mm drills
- Nail scissors
- Knife
- Sanding stick
- Needle files
- Filler

Materials:

- Ratio SR/BR loading gauge, cat. 412
- Length of very thin wire
- 40 × 40-thou plastic strip

METHOD

Remove the post from the kit sprue and clean off any flash. Note that the prototype post is cast with a separate horizontal section. In reality the joint for this is quite prominent, so don't file it flat. Then remove the two bump-bar pieces and join them with solvent so they form one solid piece. When fully set, fill the holes with model filler or Tipp-Ex, and sand flat when fully dry. Also fill the three holes in the top of the post. Find the centre of the bar and drill two 0.5mm holes in the face of the bar 8mm each side of this centre point.

Drill a 0.6mm hole at the end of a length of 40 × 40 square strip. Round off the end with sanding stick, and cut to a length of 3mm at an angle of 45

degrees. Repeat this twice more. Fix these three pieces to the top of the post 3mm from each end and in the centre. The wire included in the kit should be threaded through, but it may be easier to thread first, and then stick. Cut two of the small double-ended link pieces from the sprue, and thread these on to the wire set at 16mm apart to form the lifting outriggers. You could trim the wire at this point, or use it as a handle for the time being.

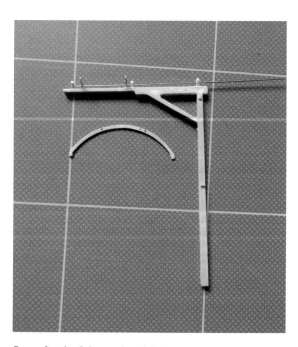

Parts finished: bump bar filled and re-drilled, bar fitted to the top, and outriggers from the kit parts. Thin wire must be added.

Cut two lengths of the finest wire you can find. I used a single piece of multi-core layout wire with the insulation stripped off. Then use this wire to tie the two outrigger parts to the bump bar. This is quite difficult to do, and it may take a couple of attempts to get it all together. Decide at this point at what height you want the bar: try it against a piece of track and a large vehicle. Finally the same thin wire can be used to run down the post from the top bar to a point about 20mm from the foot to represent the operating cable.

Note that the use of Blu-tack is almost compulsory for holding the post in different positions during the build.

IN CONCLUSION

With all the above small projects it is not really necessary to make all these modifications. However, it is worth repeating yet again that while we are fortunate to have a multitude of kits and parts in every model shop, even the smallest item needs to be assessed for its usefulness and accuracy. Don't just accept that what is marked on the packet is typical or correct.

This is particularly important for the branch-line modeller, because even up to the end of steam (and as many of the photos show, even more recently) there are many remnants of earlier ages: things did not simply change overnight with each new ownership period. It is therefore important when looking at Southern Region period photos to concentrate not just on the rolling stock but to look into the middle distance and assess the small lineside items as well. Are the signals of pre-group designs, or new? Is the platelayers' hut an original wooden one,

Complete, but non-adjusted post. The wire here needs to be shortened to raise the bump bar up a few millimetres. Note the use of Blu-tack to hold the post in place throughout the build.

or a Southern concrete replacement? Or as in many cases, have the older items been modified with new parts – for instance, new arms on old signal posts?

It is these tiny details that will add character and give the correct flavour to your layout, and prevent it being an identikit copy of all the other layouts whose owners have added items without question because that's what the packet said to do, with no reference to the real thing.

CHAPTER SEVEN

NON-REVENUE-EARNING VEHICLES

Non-revenue vehicles are the most ignored part of the railway. The reasons for this are fairly clear: for the railway itself they are the items that don't generate any profit, only being there for safety and maintenance purposes. And for the modeller and enthusiast they are the least romantic and exciting pieces of rolling stock, a long way behind any locomotives or coaches – though of course proto-typically they are highly necessary for the running of the system. Such vehicles would include ballast wagons, tamping machines, tool vans, barrier wagons and of course the humble brake van, carrying nothing but the guard, lamps and detonators at the rear. The reasons for such vehicles are obvious, but for the modeller they fall way down the list of items to buy or build – but like the signals discussed earlier, they are critical, and in some ways should be factored in fairly early in any new layout planning.

BRAKE VANS

It is probably worth spending a minute or two

Even-plank 25-ton 'Pillbox' brake van at Swanage. The van has been modified with air receivers on the balcony and a drainpipe in the side, though it still carries sandboxes.

looking at what brake vans do. Don't think you can ignore them: if you have only one loco and one wagon, then you need a brake van next. The brake van (or to use the earlier designation, 'break') does three things: first, it carries the guard who is primarily the eyes of the driver at the rear of the train, and who is there to protect the rear of the train in case of a problem, by warning any train approaching from the rear that there may be an obstruction (technically it is the guard's train and not the driver's, and hence the name 'guard' as opposed to the American 'brakeman'). This rear protection would be achieved by attaching small explosive devices (detonators) to the rail and by the use of flags.

Second, at its most basic the van will have a manual brake. This is used for controlling the speed of a train and keeping the couplings tight on a loose-coupled train. And third, using its earlier and cruder terminology 'break', it is the last resort if a coupling snaps and the train 'breaks', because the manual brake could then slow, stop and retain the

loose wagons. A lot of the above applied more to nineteenth-century usage, and with the coming of continuous braking systems, first by vacuum, then air, the role of the brake van decreased, although loose 'unfitted' trains were still common up until the 1960s.

In short, if you are modelling the earlier Southern Region period you will definitely need a brake van, but post-1968 its use is dependent on the type of goods train and how it is braked. There are all sorts of operational wildcards as well. For example, a brake van may still be used on a fully air-braked train that wouldn't seem to need one, because if an awkward reversing manoeuvre is involved, the guard once again becomes the driver's eyes at the rear (now the front) of the train, and would signal to the driver via flags and whistle whether or not the road ahead was safe.

WHICH BRAKE VAN?

As with all the rolling stock discussed in earlier chapters, there is a historical set of considerations. At its inception the Southern Railway took over a large number of pre-grouping company brake vans. Many of these survived in minor roles until quite late, and several ended up on the Isle of Wight, but the immediate push for standardization where possible led the Southern Railway to build a set of new designs. However, before this took place the Southern briefly built a small number of SECR-designed 'Dancehall' vans, and an express bogie design, not untypically recycling the underframes of LBSCR electric-motor luggage vans to do so.

The classic Southern Railway van is the 'Pillbox'. Built from 1928 to 1946, these four-wheeled brake vans had a cabin that was little more than half the size of the Dancehalls (which may account for the common name, indicating the tiny size) and to a weight rating of 25 tons. Variants were ongoing, and the modeller needs to decide exactly which van to copy as the differences are wide ranging, with a look-out ducket that moved from the left to the right (as you face the side), two types of planking style, and post-war, the addition of end windows –

TIP: STUDY TRAIN CONSISTS FOR THE PERIOD YOU ARE MODELLING

Study train consists for the period you are modelling, and look at when, where and how a brake van is used, and why this may be. Is there a van? Where is it in the train? What is its purpose in this instance? Of course once you start doing this, then you open up a hornet's nest, and simple questions become complex questions. This is why some railway modellers turn into fact-finding historians and the modelling becomes secondary, as the knowledge gained gradually becomes more important. These modellers often produce layouts that are highly accurate with regard to operating procedures, but are less scenically developed, as anything beyond the railway fence is not as interesting.

SECR-designed 'Dancehall' brake van at Horsted Keynes. The footboards and axle boxes have been altered, but otherwise this is a standard product.

Uneven-plank Pillbox at Cottesmore. Again air receivers are fitted, and again the sandboxes remain. Note that it is rated 20 tons.

The BR replacement: standard BR 20-ton van built at Darlington in 1952 and photographed at Oakworth.

and that's before the different braking and sanding arrangements are thought of. Although ubiquitous, the Pillboxes were not universally popular, being cramped and initially having the door opening into the only space where you could sit (hence the position of the ducket being moved from left to right to alleviate this).

The last Southern developments were a lighter weight, 15-ton version of the Pillbox with shallower solebars for lighter branch-line usage, and a new bogie version for express working, but like the original Pillboxes rated at 25 tons. Even though the overall length of these express vans was over 36 feet, as compared to the 24 feet of the four wheelers, in true economical form the Southern Railway kept the small cabin but fitted double-length open balconies – meaning the guard could either freeze

outside with more legroom than he'd ever need, or swelter in the tiny cramped cabin.

THE BRITISH RAILWAYS (SOUTHERN) BRAKE VAN: TRAPS AND OPTIONS

Once the region was nationalized two things happened, and this is where the trap lies for the modeller who aspires to an accurate scene. First, the brake-van fleet was analysed and yet again found to be non-standard by BR. This meant that the new standard British Railways brake van, which was a development of a London and North Eastern Railway design, became the preferred van under the then new modernization plan.

Second, as the freight workings reduced dramati-

The other likely contender: a BR (Midland Region) van. Many of these were sent south as the freight traffic was eased off the railway in the 1950s and 1960s.

cally throughout the whole British system, more vans became available from more northern areas, and more importantly these were bigger vans. This would probably have been very popular with crews, because in comparison with the Pillboxes, the accommodation provided by these interlopers was positively luxurious, though the ride quality was apparently lacking. By the time the pick-up freight train was phased out in the mid-1960s, the Pillboxes had been all but pushed out, either scrapped or moved to departmental use.

What this means for the modeller is that, once again, what he might expect is not the prototype actuality. Even a cursory study of freight on the Southern Region shows that during the 1950s and 1960s the Pillbox designs were quite scarce, and the reality was that most workings now carried a pure BR or ex-London Midland Railway van at the rear.

Once again for the modeller there is a choice: the obvious and logical, or the actual and prototypical.

PROJECT THIRTEEN: BUILDING THE PILLBOX BRAKE

Tools:
- Knife
- Sanding stick
- Needle files
- 1.5, 1 and 0.5mm drills
- Solvent

Materials:
- Cambrian SR 25-ton brake van, ref. C7
- 1mm plastic rod
- Weight
- Glazing material

25-ton brake-van underframe. The crudely added rod gives the impression of the handbrake linkage.

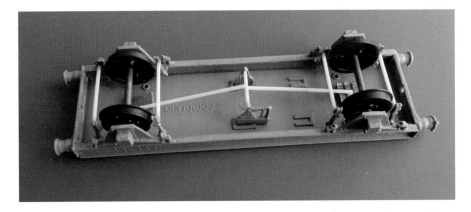

Sometimes there are ready-to-run, 25-ton Pillbox and Queen Mary brake vans that are available through the trade. Supply is variable, however, so it is logical to look at the fairly long-lived kit from Cambrian.

METHOD

The kit can be built following the instructions, which will give you a Southern Railway version or the British Railways version, but a couple of alterations need to be carried out. The first thing to tackle is the floor. After cleaning up the part, four holes need to be drilled with a 1mm drill at the points marked. The Southern fitted a large, V-shaped sandbox on each platform, but on many vans these were removed by British Railways, leaving holes in the floor where the sandpipes ran through.

The instructions state that the solebars and buffer beams should be constructed first and then the floor added. However, this is bad practice and is likely to result in a twisted underframe. Instead, insert the axle bearings, which are a push fit, and add the solebars to the floor one at a time, making sure that both are level and that the axles are completely parallel. The kit differs from most plastic vehicle kits by having a bevel joint here, rather than the solebar sitting flat on the bottom of the floor. Make sure that this gives a true and level running unit that doesn't rock, and test it through a point if you have one available. Note that the solebars sit just outside the floor edge-line with a very slight lip. Only when you are happy with this assembly should you add the buffer beams.

The raised detail needs to be filed off the edges. Note the orientation. Keep the opening to the left for a right-hand ducket van.

Note that the plating on the balcony end floor sits a little higher that you would expect. There will probably be one or two gaps in the finished assembly, which can be filled with some scrap microstrip. Brake-shoe transverse link rods can be added from 1mm plastic rod, as with previous projects. What I have also done is add similar rod along the general line of the handbrake assembly, to where each set of brake yokes would sit inside each wheelset. This is a long way from accurate, and will be largely hidden behind the footsteps, but what it does is give some visual representation that there is something going on underneath. By the time the underframe is painted it creates just enough information to suggest something more complicated. Of course you could go the whole way and add the propeller bracket on

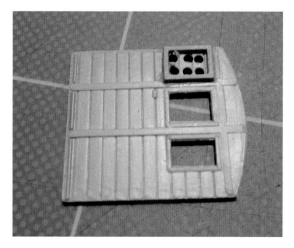

Window-frame added and holes drilled to open out the centre.

the centre rod and the yokes if you so desire.

Decide which way round the body sides go, and mark the inner surface 'inside' in pencil. In order for the inner ends to fit flush, all rivet detail and corner plates need to be filed off the inside leading edges with a flat needle file. This is a right-hand ducket van so the opening needs to be on the left for both sides while you carry this out. This is where the mistake is likely to be made, so double check that you have the correct planking (here the even type) and the correct orientation before you start filing.

Then drill the six holes per side 0.5mm to take the handrails. Again, fitting these at this point is not what the instructions say, but is easier to do when the parts are flat.

Add the duckets, then all the handrails from 0.5mm wire using the 'long leg, short leg' method – bending one leg of the rail to the depth of the plastic plus the gap, and leaving the other long to give a handle. Superglue the wire into the holes using a piece of card as a spacer, and trim off the excess on the inside using side cutters. This method is much easier than scrabbling around on the inside of a vehicle after the body has been built.

As built, the Pillbox van had only one window at each end plus the door, but British Railways added either one or two more windows on either side of this existing pair. Stick the frames provided with the kit to the end, then carefully chain-drill a series of holes around the inside of the frame, join them with a knife, and push the middle out. The resulting hole can then be filed back to the frame inside edge with a needle file.

When both ends are finished the cabin can be constructed, with the ends set inside the sides. Note that the sides are about 1mm lower than the ends.

Most of the photos of the Pillbox vans show at least one balcony gate left open. This is easily repli-

Pieces of lead sheet are added to the floor of the cabin, and the entire inside is painted black before the glazing is added.

cated by setting the door moulding at an angle when fixing it to the outer ends. Note that the pair of tabs on the door mouldings are just to locate against the inner ends, so if set in the open position, these need to be removed with a file or sanding stick. Also be aware that there are several different door parts in the kit, so take care to get the right one, and fit them the right way around – in this case the wide horizontal planking needs to be facing outwards.

When the cabin section has been fitted, add some weight – here I've used lead sheet trapped against the floor using some scrap plastic – then paint the whole of the inside a dark shade to kill any light, though wait until the outside has been painted before adding glazing material.

The rest of the build should more or less follow the instructions. A final detail could be to add the battens that marked the inside edges of the original placement of the sandboxes, which appear in some photos. This could be from 1mm channel plastic strip, or 40-thou square strip about 4mm long.

The van's livery went through several stages under BR. The unfitted vans started in pale grey, and the vacuum-fitted examples in bauxite until they were transferred into departmental use, when they became dark olive green or black. Here, Humbrol 64 was used for the bodywork and 67 dark grey for the underframe. The van has been lightly 'weathered' with a mix of browns and greys. Transfers are waterslides from the Modelmaster range.

TIP: LOOK AT THE STORAGE LINES

When visiting preserved lines try to get away from the passenger area and take a good look at the storage lines. After checking that it is all right to do this, take a camera and look for rolling stock items, such as the above van, that are tucked away, and photograph these from several angles. Much of the freight stock on preserved railways is simply stored and is never likely to see the light of day in a public arena, so take multiple shots of every small detail. Take care, and remember you may need permission to do this.

The complete Pillbox in 'unfitted' BR grey.

CHAPTER EIGHT

SOUTHERN REGION STEAM-HAULED COACHES

As discussed right at the beginning of the book, the Southern Region was primarily a passenger hauler, with less freight than the other BR regions. What it also did differently was to run a system of dedicated third-rail electric stock. This will be dealt with in the following chapters – but first a brief look at the steam-hauled passenger stock.

THE OLD DESIGNS

Once again it is necessary to reach right back to pre-grouping, pre-1923 days to learn the full story.

The Southern Railway was made up from companies that had fairly short route mileage (the LSWR aside). Therefore in general terms these companies built carriage stock with the following characteristics: they were short, quite densely seated, lacked on-board toilets, and were laid out in compartment style; the sides were a line of doors, one into each compartment, allowing the quick loading and unloading of passengers. These were railway systems designed not necessarily for comfort, but for fast turnaround, high volume commuter traffic with an accent on a straightforward, efficient travel-

Ex-SECR 'birdcage' brake as preserved at Tenterden. These were designed for the Kent lines with limited width restrictions. This did not allow the use of side duckets for the guard; instead the lookouts went up, looking over the roof. Due to these restrictions, the vehicles were long-lived and were still used on Eastern section branch-line service right into the 1960s.

ling service, in some ways predicting the way that air travel would develop in the late twentieth century, beginning with high comfort luxury, followed by high density cheap travel.

The Southern Railway thus inherited a set of stock that was specifically designed for purpose, and of course two of the pre-group lines had experimented with electric power: the LSWR with third rail pick-up and the LBSCR with an overhead system. Therefore the Southern Railway was already in the mindset of going down this particular route, so given that the existing stock was suitable for the job in hand and that it would presumably be replaced by electric stock in due course, there seemed little point in replacing it with newly designed stock with similar characteristics; so aside from rebuilds, the Southern Railway built no pure compartment carriages. The idea was to increase the corridor variety for use on longer routes and cascade these down from mainline use as these lines were electrified, while the pre-group, non-corridor panelled carriage stock would be replaced and scrapped as soon as possible. That was the plan, but unfortunately it was upset by the war.

THE NEW DESIGNS

What the Southern very quickly developed was a line of corridor coaches, first under R. Maunsell and then under O. Bulleid, the Southern's chief mechanical engineers. This was partly to fill the gap as above, but they also had an eye on the competing routes west with the Great Western Railway, a company with fewer but slightly more luxurious and comfortable carriage stock.

The Maunsell designs were outwardly quite traditional. Bulleid's, however, were more radical, moving right away from the wood panelling and multiple doors and, echoing other company's stock, shifting to the use of curved steel sheet, modern rounded windows, and doors at each end, feeding a full-length corridor. This is, of course, greatly simplifying a very complex development process and a bewildering set of coach designs, built with three different line width restrictions, over a twenty-five

year period. It is recommended that if you wish to learn more, search out the books of Mike King, who has written extensively on the Southern Railway's carriage histories.

World War II was a significant influence. Not only was the Southern Railway in the front line and received considerable wear and bomb damage, but the grand electrification plans were put on hold and were not really started again until the 1950s. This combination of circumstances led to a further batch of Bulleid designs being built from 1946 at both Eastleigh and at Birmingham, the Eastleigh building continuing into Southern Region days in 1951.

ENTERING BRITISH RAILWAYS (SOUTHERN)

By way of summary for the BR(S) modeller: you are free to do as you please with carriage stock – that is, as long as you stick to the rules. Instead of the brave new world that was envisaged in the 1930s with clean electricity, BR(S) was forced to continue with steam haulage throughout the old Southern system. What that meant was that despite the planned cascading of new corridor stock, there were still quite a number of pre-group designs working secondary and branch lines at nationalization. Many of these had been converted to push-pull units, or, as the Southern Railway contrarily defined them, 'pull-push' (push-pull units are a single or two carriages attached to a suitably fitted locomotive that hauls as normal in one direction, but pushes from the rear on the return, removing the need to run round; the driver would sit in a cab in the leading coach operating the regulator via a set of rods, while the fireman coaled the engine and applied the brake).

In many cases these push-pull units continued to work the branches until closure and were never replaced. Loose pre-group carriages were also to be found on some rural branches up until the 1960s, such as the SECR 'birdcage' units on the Tenterden branch, though in some ways these were rare birds. Most non-Bulleid coaches were quickly replaced either by the newer Southern-built stock or by the

1947-built Bulleid CK carriage 5768 undergoing overhaul at the Bluebell Railway's carriage shop.

new BR Mark 1 designs, but by the late 1950s with new electrification stock cascading, they were all but gone.

For the modeller of BR(S) there is a nominal cut-off. If you are modelling one of the short branches up to 1959 you can just about get away with pre-group designs in British Railways liveries, but after that you are slightly pushing your luck and credibility, as even the shortest lines were often using Bulleids and Mark 1s. There are many photos of wide-bodied first-phase Bulleids towering over a tiny Terrier locomotive on the Hayling Island branch by 1960.

The BR Mark 1 coach designs were constructed in two main batches between 1951 and 1964. These were incredibly long-lived, and the electric multiple-unit versions were to be seen throughout the Southern Region until 2004. The Mark 2 designs were built from 1964 to 1975. These developments

really sounded the death knell for the Bulleids: BR(S) had introduced Mark 1-influenced diesel multiple units on most non-electrified secondary lines, and the system had shrunk in the west either by closure, or because the remaining lines west of Salisbury were handed over to the BR Western Region.

The final piece in the plan slotted into place when the line to Bournemouth was electrified. This essentially removed the need for any large quantity of locomotive-hauled stock on the Southern Region, and most (but not all) of the SR's carriage stock was scrapped or stored. This decision did in some ways prove to be its saviour, because if it had been retained it would have been worked out and withdrawn, and cannibalized by BR. As it turned out, it provided a set of relatively new, low mileage rolling stock for the preservation movement, much of which is Bulleid, stocked on the south's several heritage lines.

A Class 73 powers through Ashford in the 1980s, running off the third rail electric pick-up with a train of Pullman coaches of the Orient Express.

By the 1970s the 1930s transformation plan was virtually complete. Nearly all BR(S) was unit run, most was electric, and only the new western extremity had anything resembling a hauled train, with Class 50s, consists such as the Class 33 with TC (Trailer Control) and RES (Restraint) push-pull trains, and some Kent coast boat trains.

The final consideration is the make-up of trains. Although the Southern Railway did produce 'loose' carriages, most of the build planning was to produce fixed rakes of varying lengths, referred to as 'sets'. These sets could be anything from three car – brake-open-brake – to ten car sets, including 'tavern cars' and/or Pullman cars. Lists of the construction and numbering of these sets are available online, but be ready for this to take a long time as not only are they very extensive, but they do not always tally. This may be in part due to the compilers, but the situa-

tion is not helped by the SR having wilfully moved vehicles around between different sets, obviously wishing to confuse the future rail historian. The use of these sets was continued by BR(S), and the number of each set was usefully denoted on the end of each unit by large white or cream numerals.

TIP: INVEST IN A FEW PICTURE ALBUM BOOKS

Before you buy any coaches, invest in a few picture album-type books and look at the spread of designs for the period you wish to represent. It's unlikely that what you *thought* would be used is actually what was used, especially post-1959.

LIVERIES

At nationalization British Railways tried a number of colour schemes for carriage stock, settling on crimson and cream, or plain crimson for pure suburban non-corridor stock. In time, most of the existing Southern Region stock was repainted into these colours. In 1956 the painting rules were relaxed and the regions were permitted to revert to the old company paint schemes, and the Southern Region changed mainline stock to a green similar to the malachite of the earlier pre-nationalization years. This green coach policy has become so ingrained in public consciousness that green is still the colour that most still associate with BR(S) carriages of the period, even though a faded crimson could be dominant on secondary lines.

NEW BRITISH RAILWAYS COACH DESIGNS

In 1951 the production of the first new British Railways Mark 1 standard coach designs was commenced. These, while not exactly groundbreaking, and following much of the later-day styles of the grouping companies' products, were a departure in that they were country-wide vehicles – almost. Due to the reasons given earlier, much of the Kent traffic still had to reach back to pre-group designs as the new Mark 1s were simply too wide for the compact loading gauge.

The Mark 1s were first liveried in crimson and cream, then green on BR(S), and maroon elsewhere in the country. The upshot of all this repainting was that mainline trains could include vehicles of several different colours. The designs were very long-lived, much longer than those they replaced, the last being withdrawn in 1999, and the associated electric multiple unit (EMU) versions were not officially cleared until 2004. This means that the Mark 1 is undoubtedly the most successful passenger-carrying design in British history, if age is the determining factor.

In 1964 the building programme shifted to the Mark 2 designs, and with it a new colour scheme of blue and grey. The Mark 1 stock followed suit,

Restored Southern Region 9269 Mark 1 at Tenterden.

TIP: NOTE THAT CARRIAGE STOCK LIVERY VARIES

In general, carriage stock livery is green. However, do bear in mind that repainting was not a high priority, and branch-line stock would often be in crimson until quite late, and cascaded ex-mainline would already be in green, so a mix is likely. Push-pull stock rarely came out of crimson. By the time 'rail blue' was introduced in 1964, most of the branches had either been closed or dieselized with multiple units.

but as anything older was due for withdrawal, the Southern green stayed until the end of steam on the region. Slow painting schedules being what they are, though, meant that the green and maroon was still to be seen into the 1970s.

READY-TO-RUN PASSENGER STOCK

If you are working in 4mm scale then there is much to be grateful for. Bachmann introduced three Bulleid designs some twenty years ago that were applauded at the time, though very soon these were outstripped by new, improved production techniques. Now the quality of ready-to-run vehicles is unbelievably high and there is little for the modeller to do. For the gaps in the ready-to-run products there are still kits available from Ian Kirk (Cooper Craft), and if you require pre-group designs then Roxey Mouldings produce a range of LBSCR and LSWR models – useful if you wish to run push-pull trains. For the ambitious, the 'scratch-aid' kits from Worsely Works consist of a huge range of brass sides and ends for many pre-group vehicles that lasted into BR days.

For the novice, the Bachmann Bulleids are a good starting point, and are available second-hand and new at favourable prices – often half the amount of the newer coaches. As mentioned above, the

models were quickly superseded: most of the complaint was that they lacked flush glazed windows. This can be replaced, with commercial items such as those from South East Finecast, but the fitting is very tricky and many will not see the point. Quite honestly, if you want a set of sound, robust BR(S) vehicles to start your fleet, then the Bachmann models are a good first choice. Extra to this, you can improve them in small ways with a little modelling.

PROJECT FOURTEEN: THE BACHMANN BRAKE THIRD

Aside from the glazing issue mentioned above, in this project most of the work is cosmetic. The following is a basic set of ideas, and is far from comprehensive – for example, the roof could have better cast fittings added, and a wire handrail could be fitted at the end, and so on. What the next three or four steps will do is build the modeller's confidence, and give a vehicle that is a little more personal than a straight out-of-the-box item.

Tools required:
- Small flat screwdriver
- Sanding stick
- Solvent

Materials required:
- Paint
- Transfers: Fox ref. FRH 4008

The vehicle is in three parts: the underframe and bogies, the body and roof moulding, and the interior moulding. The body can be pulled off or prised off with a flat screwdriver.

THE INTERIOR

The interior section is a piece of shiny brown plastic, and this is where a lot of the visual improvement can quickly be made. First it needs toning down a little, and second it needs a little colour variation – not enough to make it jump out at the viewer, but just enough to stop it looking like a piece of plastic. A study of interior photos suggests that there were

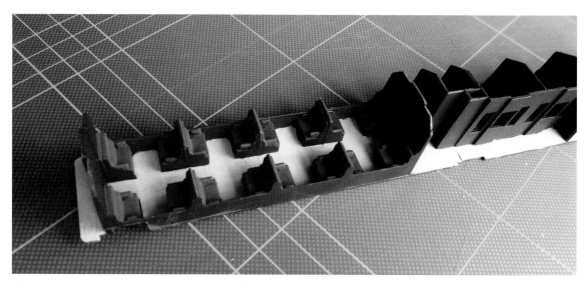

The plastic interior can be painted in simple block colours.

variables in fitting out, even within the same class of vehicle. This is possibly due to the availability of material: these were carriages built at the height of rationing, and presumably fabric and so on would have been subject to the same shortages as most other things. However, the overriding colours are pale blue or duck-egg flooring and russet colours for seating. This conclusion is not definitive, but is probable.

The floor sections were painted with Humbrol 90, which many people will have over from painting the underside of Airfix Spitfires. The seats themselves were painted with Humbrol 70, and the rest of the plastic was painted with Games Workshop 'Skrag Brown'. This is not highly detailed, involved paintwork, just blocks of colour to give the impression of different areas through the window. This would work for any of the three Bachmann carriages; the only additional task is to paint the luggage compartment cream. If you wished, this could be highly detailed with a desk, mirror, hanging jacket and lamps in the guard's section.

*Typical guards compartment,
here in a Mark I brake.*

The inside of the roof was also painted with two coats of Humbrol 90 to reflect a little light down into the compartments, and a couple of human figures were added. You could do much more: most compartments had either pictures or mirrors at the ends, and there were, of course, luggage racks. Either of these is possible, but it is questionable if you would be able to see them enough to make it a worthwhile exercise.

THE BODY

Most coaches during the period were kept reasonably clean – the sides, anyway. These were either hand washed or the carriage was put through the automatic washers. What did remain fairly grimy were the ends and underframe, both of which would develop a coating of brake dust and general dirt thrown up from the rails. The ends of the model are painted black, which is ideal, but unlikely. A fast way to improve the body is to paint the ends a dirty dark grey: here I've used Games Workshop 'Charadon Granite', which has a brown tone in it.

As explained above, the SR and BR(S) grouped most carriages in 'sets' with additional 'loose' vehicles, which could be added or detached at will to strengthen a train or replace a crippled unit. This particular model is numbered 3955, which makes it an Eastliegh-built vehicle originally destined for 'loose' use, but which was then included in a three-car set, 769. This particular set started work in North Kent, was transferred to the Oxted line, then lastly moved west, making it useful for the modeller as it could have been seen in the East, West or Central sections.

The set number needs to be put on the outer luggage section end, one three-digit number on either side of the corridor connections. Specific coach-numbering transfers are available, but if you are planning to finish a steam locomotive or two, then the sheet indicated is designed for this but includes smaller numbers that are suitable for the carriage sets.

When this work on the body has been completed, the interior piece can now be clipped back inside, making sure that it is the right way around.

ASSEMBLING THE BODY AND UNDERFRAME

For lining-up purposes the body can now be loosely attached to the underframe. The model should include a set of footstep parts for you add, but if it doesn't, these can easily be made from 4mm-wide strips of 30-thou plastic sheet. The footstep positions varied between batches and due to repairs, but essentially you will require one short step under each passenger door, and longer steps under the guard/luggage doors. These also require a step on the bogie frame below, set level, and between the axle boxes. These can be fixed using solvent, but be careful not to get any on to the surface of the body side, as it will strip the finish in a second.

Set numbers applied using Fox transfers. The end has been painted dark grey to tone down the black plastic.

Bogies can be toned down using a mix of greys and rust colours to represent dirt and brake dust.

The underframe can now be removed and painted as a whole, using the same approach as the wagons dealt with earlier, using a mix of dark grey and rust tones. Finally clip the body back on to the underframe, and lightly weather if desired.

The same type of process can be used for any BR(S) vehicle from pregroup through to the Mark 1 and 2 stock.

TIP: DON'T DISCOUNT USING SLIGHTLY OLDER MODELS

Don't discount using slightly older models such as this one. They were considered first rate in their day, and can still hold their own against newer productions. The trick is to produce a consistent overall finish throughout your fleet. We interact with our models on a visual level, and this consistent finish will usually smooth out differences in the ages of the models and the quality of the manufacture. We only actually see the final coat of paint, not the levels below.

The completed Bulleid brake third.

CHAPTER NINE

INTO MODERNIZATION – A SIMPLE LOCOMOTIVE KIT-BUILD

America and parts of Europe had started to dieselize mainline locomotive fleets from the early 1940s; Britain, however, hung on grimly to steam for another two and half decades. Part of the reason has been discussed earlier: finance, war and union strength, but that is not to say that the desire was not there. The pre-war Southern Railway was keen to move forwards: parts of the system had already been electrified with third rail pick-up, and the company looked towards diesel power for the small amount of freight haulage.

THE MAUNSELL SHUNTER

One of the first ideas to come to fruition was a small shunting engine. This could be started instantly and put to work, avoiding the long process of being coaled and brought to steam every morning, wasting valuable man hours. The diesel shunter could also likely be operated all day without any further fuelling or maintenance to be carried out. For these points alone it is easy to see why all the railway companies had a desire to move towards diesel traction and reduce the more costly steam locomotive running costs.

The chief mechanical engineer R. E. Maunsell is usually credited with the design, though there is some doubt as to whether he actually had a hand in it, or whether it is often referred to as 'the Maunsell shunter' purely as he was in charge at the time. Also, the other three grouping companies adopted almost identical designs during the same period, which suggests that this was a general development by the many industrial locomotive builders of the time, and the design was simply copied and adopted by the mainline companies. Regardless of that, the Southern Railway did produce three identical 0-6-0

locomotives in 1937, which lasted in service until 1964.

It will quickly be noticed that the locomotive bears a resemblance to the later English Electric 350hp shunter (later Class 08), which became the standard BR small, all-purpose machine built from 1953 and is still with us – though this was slightly closer to the London Midland Scottish Railway machine. Where the Southern locomotive differs slightly from all these, including the 08, was in its racy performance: all the others limped along at a pedestrian 17–20mph (27–30km/h), while the Maunsell shunter was a thoroughbred with a galloping 30mph (50km/h) top speed. What this meant in reality was that it was not limited purely to yard shunting work and could be used for trip freight work on the mainline.

In the 1940s the Maunsell diesels were used for War Department work towing guns, but at nationalization BR(S) renumbered the trio 15201–3 and settled them working around Norwood Junction and the Central Section. By the 1960s they were worked out and were replaced by BR first-generation diesel locomotives such as the Class 33 and the aforementioned English Electric Class 08.

- -
PROJECT FIFTEEN: BUILDING THE MAUNSELL SHUNTER
- -

One area where the novice modeller may struggle is the jump from shop-bought ready-to-run locomotives to kit-built examples. Much of the fear involved comes from the lack of experience in soldering brass and nickel-silver parts, and producing a well-running chassis. But by using one of the many resin body kits that can be mounted on a ready-to-run chassis unit, confidence can be slowly built up, and even if your work is not top quality to start with, at least it will run well due to the commercial running gear. Golden Arrow Models produce such a kit for the Maunsell shunter, which can be built easily and reasonably quickly into a great looking and well running alternative to the ubiquitous Class 08 for the Southern Region layout.

Tools required:
- Pin chuck and small drills
- Needle files and one larger size file
- Razor saw

Materials required:
- Golden Arrow Models Maunsell 1937 shunter kit
- Bachmann 08 diesel (any livery and condition as long as it runs)
- 0.5 brass wire (or similar)
- Signal ladder: 3mm Scale Model Railways ref. S114 (or similar)
- 40-thou square plastic strip
- Epoxy resin adhesive (the cheap variety from pound shops is more than adequate)

- Gel-type superglue
- Filler
- Paint/transfers

CLEANING UP

As can be seen, the kit includes a handful of creamy resin parts. Most of the bodyshell is already made, with just ends, top and doors to add. In common with most kits made from this material there is quite a bit of 'flash' to be cleaned off, as the moulding process used is cruder than the plastic injection process of the wagon kits of earlier chapters, and usually uses rubber moulds rather than precision metal tooling. Therefore the first job is to roughly clean up all the parts included.

GETTING THE BODY TOGETHER

The end part drops in between the sides, which flex out a little. This is probably the longest part of the build: getting the sides parallel by shaving the end part a little, and carving the sides out slightly until a good clean fit is obtained. Take your time through this section, and have some sort of light clamping

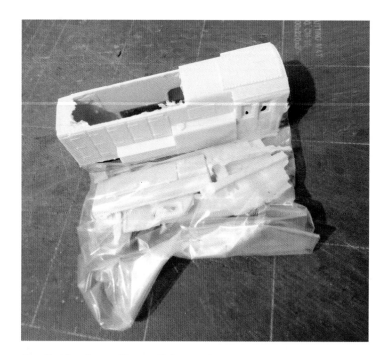

The Golden Arrow Maunsell shunter kit as supplied.

TIP: DON'T BE TOO PRECISE WITH THE CLEAN-UP

Don't be too precise with the clean-up as there is an amount of fettling involved to get the parts to fit well – leave yourself enough material to do this. It's easy to take off too much, and you can't put it back. Just get off most of the thin wispy flash and do the detailed cleaning as you start to fit the parts together.

Material needs to be removed from the underside of the bonnet top in order to clear the motor.

The rear end needs to be fettled to fit and the sides squeezed in while the adhesive 'goes off'.

device such as a vice or small G-clamp to hand, to hold the part while the epoxy sets. A small amount of filler may also be necessary to make the final set joint smooth.

CHASSIS MODIFICATION

With the end on, the chassis rear can be trimmed with a razor saw, according to the instructions, to suit the curve at the bottom of the cab. This is the anxious period for the novice, as his ingrained desire will be not wanting to ruin what is a perfectly good working model. Be brave, however: the length to cut away will be a little over 20mm. 40-thou strip can now be added along the outside of the Bachmann footplate to bring it out level with the tanks and toolbox, butting up tight against the curve of the cab foot.

As well as rounding the corners of the vertical circuit board to clear the inside of the radiator, the inside of the bonnet cover also needs to be thinned

down by a millimetre or two to clear the motor. This can easily be done using a large file, as shown.

THE DOOR GRAB HANDLES

A line of holes can now be drilled with a 0.6mm drill – two at the top of each door 6mm from the top, and on the long doors 6mm from the bottom. The holes should be spaced 6mm apart for the upper pairs and 3mm apart for the lower. Add the handrails (actually door handles in this case) from 0.5mm wire fixed with superglue on the inside. When fully set, gently file off any excess wire inside so that it doesn't foul the mechanism.

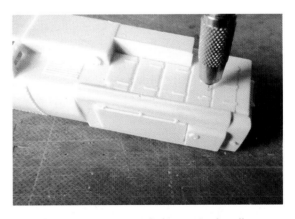

The engine compartment doors require handles to be fitted using wire. Here the holes are being drilled with a pin chuck and 0.6mm drill bit.

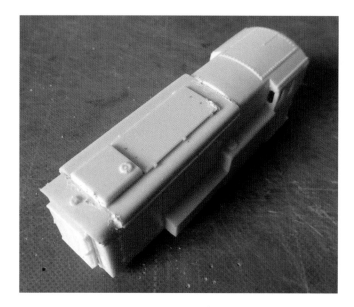

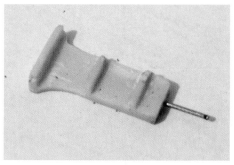

ABOVE: *The rear cab steps benefit from having extra support in the shape of a length of wire.*

LEFT: *The basic body assembled with a little filler applied prior to cleaning up.*

Similar vertical handrails can be added on each side of the cab doors. These should be 19mm long and set 1mm up from the foot of the door.

With all the roof parts attached, add two small handles 3mm wide, centrally and 2.5mm from each end of the large bonnet cover. At this point fill any small gaps in the main bodyshell using filler, and seal the joints with a coat of black paint.

THE CAB STEPS

The rear cab steps are particularly easy to damage and knock off, and do not have a lot of surface area for glue to adhere to; therefore using just glue makes for a very weak joint. Adding a wire 'peg' into the step assembly will reinforce it. First, drill into the top of the step to a depth of 3mm, insert a scrap of wire and fix it with superglue. Line up this finished step with the bottom of the cab door and mark where the wire will go. When you are happy with the position, mark a hole and drill 0.6mm. Then fix as normal with a coat of superglue. The wire will give sideways strength where a simple butt joint between step and cab is likely to fail very quickly.

THE BONNET LADDER

Unusually the Maunsell shunters had a ladder on only one side of the bonnet. As usual with Southern freight subjects, prototype photos are quite rare, and those that do exist annoyingly mainly show the nearside and not the offside where the ladder is. Therefore a small amount of guesswork is involved as to its exact positioning.

Drill two holes 3mm apart and 1mm forward from the main bonnet cover, just as the curve of the radiator section flattens out. Trim the ladder down to approximately 35mm, leaving as much tail at each end as possible. Cut a further short section just under two rungs long, bend as shown, and stick to the first piece. Solder has been used here as it gives a very strong joint, but for those nervous about such things, using epoxy resin or superglue will do just as well.

Drop the ladder into the top holes and mark where this new support will be on the body; drill two holes and attach the ladder assembly to the bonnet using superglue.

The Bachmann 08 chassis has two tanks moulded on to the coupling mount under the front buffer beam. Remove these from the mount, and depending on your coupling choice, trim and remount transversely – here to fit either side of the standard Bachmann tension lock coupling. The prototype tank is a single complete item, but is obviously right in the way of most commercial coupling fittings, so

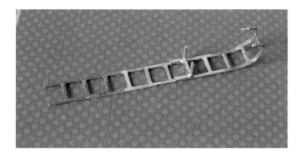

The single bonnet step unit from the brass signal ladder. The central support needs to be soldered or stuck on.

Steps in the process of being fitted.

a little suggestion is needed, and the tank is split to sit on either side.

PAINTING

The locomotive can now be painted to suit. The livery was plain black until just before withdrawal, when standard British Railways diesel green with black and yellow 'wasp' stripes was applied. Here the finished model was given a light coat of Halfords grey acrylic primer, followed by several very light coats of Tamiya Satin Black; both were applied from basic spray cans. The numbering is from the same Fox Transfer sheet as the coach-set numbering, and the British Railways logo is from the same company's range. This was followed by the weathering techniques discussed earlier, using drybrushing and washes of Humbrol acrylic from pots. The Maunsell shunters led a fairly unforgiving life, and the limited photographs show them in a rather filthy condition.

FINALLY...

Putting together a locomotive kit is very pleasurable, though of course is quite time-consuming, even with a fairly basic kit such as this. And as the ready-to-run manufacturers are unlikely to produce absolutely everything, there are always going to be gaps in the fleet to fill. Building the Maunsell shunter fills one of these gaps, and will provide a talking point for viewers of your layout.

Body kit complete and fitted to the donor Bachmann 08 chassis.

CHAPTER TEN

ELECTRIFICATION AND THE THIRD RAIL LAYOUT

DEVELOPMENT OF THE SOUTHERN ELECTRIC RAILWAY

In the early years of the twentieth century the suburbs were quickly spreading south from London. For the railway companies this was wonderful news as it heralded an almost unlimited growth in possible passengers, and they encouraged this development wholeheartedly. They did not have it all their own way, however: the much more flexible and convenient electric street tram systems were also stretching their tentacles along these new suburban roads, and the pressure was on to compete with these with a faster, more efficient service. The LBSCR was the first to move to newer technology, with an electric train system that by 1912 had reached as far south from the capital as Selhurst, with the long-term aim of reaching the coast at Brighton. The power supply used was 6,600 volts AC, fed through an overhead set of catenary wires, visually reminiscent of the 25kV systems that cover much of the United Kingdom today.

A few years later, just prior to World War I, the LSWR also found that it was being pushed into a situation where it, too, needed to electrify lines out of London, and by 1916 its electric lines had reached Claygate. The difference to the LBSCR was the method of power supply: while the Brighton company chose overhead-supplied AC, the LSWR decided on a more easily maintained, but some would say more dangerous, 600-volt DC supply, which was fed to the train via a third rail and a pick-up shoe mounted on the outside of the bogie.

Third rail insulating 'pot'.

But World War I interrupted further development of both systems, and neither stretched any further until a short spurt of work on both in 1925. By this time the Southern Railway was in overall control – albeit dominated by ex-LSWR management – and it was decided that system-wide electrification was the future of the Southern, but that one single standard way of powering electric trains should be adopted.

The power base of the LSWR within the Southern Railway's boardrooms meant that the LSWR's 600v third rail was adopted as this standard, and from this point no further new work was done on the LBSCR's forward-thinking and groundbreaking system. Sadly by 1929 the 6,600v AC overhead wires had gone – although in true Southern style the rolling stock found new uses, and many were recycled into third rail electric trailer cars and even long-wheel-base express brake-van chassis. The way forward was electricity, and that way was third rail pick-up.

SOUTH COAST OR NOT…

Converting a whole steam railway to electric power was a slow business. By 1939 the third rail had stretched into Hampshire as far as Portsmouth, and all along the south coast eastwards as far as Ore in Sussex (where, incidentally, the powered rail section still ends today; through trains to Ashford still need to be diesel powered). The Kent coastal towns fared slightly worse. The SECR was always the poor relation, and this continued, with money poured into the wealthy commuter belts of Surrey and North Hampshire but not into the industrial North Kent industrial area and the East Kent Channel ports. Although Rochester and Maidstone were reached two months before World War II, it was a full twenty years later before Dover, Sittingbourne and Ramsgate were electrically joined.

Looking back from the twenty-first century there appears to be no sense to this. Logically the ports should be joined to the capital as a primary objective, but post-war shortages intervened, and of course the Southern had ample means of shifting the slower-moving port freight in the shape of steam stock; also passenger-laden boat trains to the

ports were being handled by a sudden 1930s rush to provide larger, express-rated steam locomotives. It almost looks as though there were two factions fighting for the budget: one with a desire to create an updated steam fleet, and one that wanted to embrace modernity with a super-efficient electric system, one that could fulfil the Southern's shift to regular timings.

It is possible that despite the enthusiasm for electric power the Southern saw it as more of a purely short-trip commuter system. There was no effort to electrify any of the far west routes: these were still operated by ever more efficient Pacific class locomotives in the years approaching World War II. The lines west of Salisbury were handed over to the Western Region operation post-war, and it seems that the Southern may have had an advanced idea that this would be the case. It would be far better in business terms to concentrate on the high-volume traffic of the moneyed London commuter.

A MORE REGULAR TIMETABLE

One of the benefits of the expanding electric-powered service was the greater ease with which the timetable could be made more regular. The departure times of trains across the UK was at the least quite random, with trains timetabled to leave, for example, at twenty-three minutes past one hour, and then fifteen and forty-one minutes past the next hour. Much of this was to do with the technicalities of the steam railway: engines needed regular servicing throughout the day and possibly mid-journey, with not only coal and water needing to be added, but regular greasing and oiling all around the motion parts, some of which could be awkward and time-consuming, especially with older machines.

This was coupled with the endless business of attaching and detaching coaches to be hauled onwards, which it is easy to forget would not move on their own. This required a locomotive to appear from somewhere (or to be taken from the front of the train) to perform the shunt move and retire; all of which took time, and involved possibly quite complicated signalling moves to achieve. Even at its most basic, the train of coaches arriving at a terminus

1955 Brighton-built BR(S) Standard Class 4 starts the run-round procedure by backing away from its train. This set of moves slowed down the turnaround times and could be avoided by using electric double-ended unit stock, which was ready to return almost immediately if required.

would need to be run around and the locomotive re-attached, or probably a new locomotive brought in and joined to the departing end.

Although for the modeller and student of the system this is a fascinating set of operations, which adds to the complexities and interest of operating a model railway, in real terms for the railway company and the passenger alike it was a complication that was universally disliked. This was not only because of the costs involved, but also the time it all took, and the way that the timetables were less about actual journey times and more about the mechanical and physical working at each end and along the way. A far more efficient way to run trains was to use fixed rakes or units of passenger stock, and to dispense

with the locomotive problem altogether. This was, of course, a problem not exclusive to the Southern, but in shifting to electric power a lot of this extra shunting and stock reassembling was reduced.

STREAMLINING THE SERVICE

Just to prove again how forward thinking it was, the LSWR had started to move towards a system of regular timetabling as early as the World War I years, and this desire was continued under the control of the Southern Railway. With the introduction of entire electrified routes, the Southern could now predict working practice more easily and therefore tighten up the service and departure times into a more regular shape: it was now possible to run trains throughout the day at the same times past the hour, every hour, something that we take for granted today but which was seen as ground-breaking during the inter-war years.

Although much of this was down to the stream-lining of working practices and more efficient steam locomotives, the bulk of the improvements, espe-cially around the London and central sections, lay in the fact that as soon as an electric unit had arrived and its passengers had left, then it was in essence ready to leave immediately; there was no need for oiling round, no locomotive running around its stock and no new locomotive needed to be brought from somewhere else to attach to the departure end in the case of the larger termini. If the train needed strengthening with extra car-riages then the units could simply be made longer by attaching one or more units at either end with the minimum of fuss and with only the smallest amount of time. If a train needed to be divided, a second locomotive was not required, only a second crew, who could of course ride with the first. Although moving parts still needed to be main-tained, the number of these was greatly reduced and could, in the majority of occasions, be done outside the station environs overnight and not at the platform.

Of course the electric-powered sections of line did not exist in a bubble. The local services and the vast majority of the branch-line work and freight was still handled by independent locomotives, and this would continue until the late 1950s and in many cases right up to the end of steam. So despite the desire for a clean new system, the electric lines were still criss-crossed by branch trains, empty passenger stock workings and dirty freight locomo-tives – though looking at the advertising produced by the Southern in the pre- and post-war years, you would think that all this 'other' non-electric traffic had been brushed away overnight.

MODELLING

For the modeller there is much to be gained from this period, if nothing else, from the point of view of variety of rolling stock. The novice modeller usually ignores anything that is not a rural branch-line layout, as that is often stated as the best way to start. However, modelling a post-war Southern Region urban working model would be a great way to show the side-by-side operation of the old and the new, especially as the slightly more difficult to produce electric units are now available in ready-to-run form at reasonable prices in 4mm scale. Most modellers who portray the earlier post-war years of the Southern Region do so by building a simple rural branch-line station, usually a terminus, and an example of a possible idea for one of these was fea-tured near the beginning of the book.

The problem that most modellers have with the Southern electric scene is that they see it in isola-tion, which of course it wasn't. The system didn't appear overnight, and there was a long period of integration with the traditional steam railway that already existed. Modellers are also caught out by the fact that the working is simple and that the stock is long. This last point, while not wrong, is misleading, as in comparative terms a Southern Region 2BIL unit is not much longer than the classic Great Western Railway (GWR) locomotive and auto trailer, which is regarded by some modellers as the ultimate short branch-line train. Part of this is because this particular train unit lasted right up to the end of steam, whereas, for example, the Southern's equivalent single carriage and loco units fell into disuse early on. Most late-build GWR auto trailers were quite long – most were around 70 feet – and then you have to factor the length of the loco-motive into that.

Thus all of a sudden an electric unit such as the SR 2BIL, with its two shorter coaches and no loco-motive, looks to be a viable proposition for a branch passenger train in a small space, and of course the physical operation (or lack of it) is the same. It is true that the electric services concentrated mainly on the main lines, but some branch termini were served even quite early on – such as Seaford in 1935, and both Bognor and Littlehampton in 1938 – so running your classic branch terminus model with a two-coach electric train and steam on the

The platform end at Seaford in Sussex, one of the earliest branch electrifications. The photo was taken in 2000. The 1980s housing stands on the site of the larger of the two goods yards. The skew bridge in the distance makes an ideal scenic break for the modeller. The original LBSCR signalbox still remained at this time, albeit long switched out of use. The third rail on the right is sited away from the platform face, and is partly boarded at the point where it was likely to be walked over by staff.

freight is a real and possibly prototypical proposition. You just have to leave behind the concept of the country branch that the model press persists in selling us.

AN URBAN TERMINUS

While the idea of an electric branch terminus is a possibility, making it the classic rural idyll is unlikely. For example, the three branch termini mentioned above are all coastal resorts, and the Southern Railway would have been very aware that a fast, efficient service to them carrying large numbers of profit-generating holidaymakers from London would be advantageous to all concerned. Conversely, during the same historical period the Southern was closing or running down several other similar length branches in the area, way in advance of the Beeching axe of the 1960s.

Dr Beeching is often seen as the architect of the destruction of the branch system, but he was really only tying up a process that had begun thirty years earlier. For instance, no one would have expected – now or at the time – the Dyke branch near Brighton to fall under the third rail electrification scheme, even though it didn't close until 1938, five years after the main coast-way line that fed it was electrified. While the Dyke branch would make an excellent model for a compact steam-powered branch, possibly one that just survived into the late 1950s, the whole visual feel of it plays against that of the Southern Region's modern electric schemes: here you need something much more urban in appearance.

URBAN FOR A SMALL SPACE

If you look at any of the three electrified termini mentioned, you will conclude that they are far from compact. Like most seaside resort stations, the original designs of the Victorian age were generous, full of grandiose ideas and hope for generating a huge profit from a seaside destination that would develop once the railway had arrived, and then return any expenditure to the company many times over. This is a story that played out all over the British Isles, and the south coast fared better than most in counting the successful routes. The lines that did not do so well (and you could count two of the three here) fell into decline and were compressed in land terms over the years post-nationalization. Many had the goods yards reduced and developed into housing or industrial buildings, and this works very well for the modeller who looks to the years after World War II.

ADAPTING THE 'LOOP AND TWO' PLAN

The standard 'loop and two' plan (a run-round loop in front of a platform road and two sidings) can be adapted here. The plan is well loved by branch-line modellers of all persuasions, and has been repeated many times over many decades. Adapting this for early urban electrics is quite simple. In very basic terms, the actual stock working is more or less the same as a rural branch, so the same track plans can be used or adapted. What is different is the number of buildings as compared to the usual rather pretty rural railway. This approach was the norm for modellers forty or fifty years ago, but possibly coupled

Facing the opposite way to the previous photo. The line on the right was only used at this time for the occasional overnight stabling of units. The staff mess room stands on the far side. Beyond the end wall stands a row of single-storey post-war shops. Both third rails are situated in the centre of the track arrangement, away from possible pedestrians.

with shrinking house sizes, the rural branch as an ideal for a first layout has taken a firm hold. The other difference is the frequency of movement. The rural branch in the post-war years may have seen only four trains a day; the electrified modern branch of the same period would just as likely have had an hourly service, all day.

The primary consideration is to think in terms of a compressed and constricted site – this would be a shrinking and developing scenario with post-war freight traffic dropping, but with an upward swing in commuter traffic and a still buoyant holiday trade before private car use took full hold. The passenger trains could be swift and frequent (if it's a Saturday) and a small number of parcel trains could be run for associated luggage, and a freight with a steam engine to handle the local coal. Mixing coal with electric trains sounds odd, but that is exactly the sort of juxtaposition I am talking about: most households were still using coal until the 1960s at least – my family certainly were – so the traffic to local coalyards was healthy, but was played against the modernity of electric passenger trains. In some ways this sounds like any other branch terminus, but this is not trees and green fields, more house backs and retaining walls.

SEAFORD STATION AND LAYOUT

The foregoing photos show Seaford pictured at the turn of the century, in 2000. This is the post-1970s track layout, but it serves our purpose here very well if we assume that rationalization began slightly earlier than it did. The site is naturally compressed, with the land dropping away to salt pans and the sea to the south, and a road that is a more recent addition to the north. The station had two small goods yards at its height, one at each side of the running line. The electric stock could be any of the two car units, and the associated steam power could be a mix of small to medium locomotives, dependent on which side of the region you are portraying – though working on the Eastern side would be unlikely.

Much of what has been dealt with so far in mod-

elling terms would be ideal; there is even evidence of 0-6-0 Terriers taking single luggage vans into the station from Newhaven, which would make a perfect and yet prototypical short train, and possibly a C or C2x 0-6-0 goods locomotive pulling a handful of coal wagons into the yard.

The third rough layout plan sketch (opposite) shows how such a terminus might be laid out. In some ways this is the purest Southern Region plan of them all, because where the previous sketches have been generously influenced by the past and the pre-group era, this plan can really state the period that we are modelling without any trains appearing. The real Seaford building is an LBSCR 'Italianate' type, similar to Portslade illustrated in Chapter Five. This, of course, does reach back to pre-group designs, so it might be better to use Bishopstone, the next station down the line, or Albany Park, again both illustrated earlier, which would set the period as definitely post-war Southern Region, with a more austere brick and concrete architectural feel. To continue this modern feeling, a brick-built signal box such as that at Lancing, or the ARP box at Gomshall, may be brought into play.

The goods yard on the plan has been severely rationalized and now consists of one lonely siding approached via the bay platform. This could be bordered not by the 1980s housing pictured at the real Seaford, but by the contemporary 1950s brick-built council housing with alleys (or to use the local term, 'twittens') between the blocks. The post-war years saw a boom in social housing construction, often alongside railway lines, as the land was cheap and becoming more available as the railways rationalized.

Opposite this, on the other side of the line, stands some low-rise light industry, possibly engineering based. The central road access is lined with the rear of advertising hoardings, and the front edge drops away slightly, accentuating the Southern Region concrete huts in the centre. Small, single-storey shop units placed around the station building area also reflect the age, with small cafés, dry cleaners and suchlike. The line disappears under a brick and girder skew bridge, as in the real Seaford.

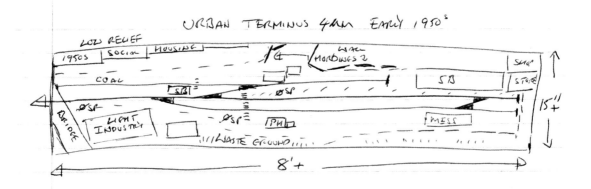

STATION BUILDING — LBSCR COASTWAY STYLE OR CONCRETE ART DECO

SIGNAL BOX — SAXBY + FARMER LBSCR TYPE OR ARP

SR PLATELAYERS HUT + TOOL HUT

STARTING SIGNALS ON RAIL-BUILT POSTS

SKEW BRIDGE OVER EXIT

'NEW' 1950s SOCIAL HOUSES AT REAR — BACKS

BRICK MESS ROOM

PECO CODE 100 TRACK

CONCRETE FENCING   SR ELECTRIC LAMPS

ONLY MAIN AND BAY PLATFORM ROADS WITH 3RD RAIL?

STOCK   c1950–59

TWO CAR UNITS 2BIL ETC

TERRIER

D1 / C / C2X

AIRFIX / DAPOL MINERAL WAGONS

CCT / PMV + VANS ON PARCELS

Rough sketch plan of a layout based on Seaford of a line set in the post-war years.

TIP: WATCH PUBLIC INFORMATION FILMS OF THE POST-WAR PERIOD

Using the internet, watch public information films and newsreels of the post-war period to gain ideas of how the scene should look beyond the railway fence. Road vehicles are key to this, but are often much older than you would think, and are still mainly pre-war designs.

This is, of course, only a basic set of ideas, and is flexible in approach. You could add another platform south of the line, and indeed make the approach double tracked. What would emphasize the changing post-electric scene is the use of the third rail only alongside the main running lines, remembering to site this in the centre of the loop away from the platform, and the post-war building styles that have swept away the pre-grouping detail. If you were standing here in 1959 this would be a very modern railway indeed.

The overall idea here is to represent the 'brave new world' of the Southern Region, where new commuter areas were being opened up, but against a feeling of austerity and a much less ostentatious and more stripped-down railway without the hopeful grandeur of the pre-group company buildings.

PROJECT SIXTEEN: MAKING THE THIRD RAIL IN 4MM SCALE

Adding a third rail to any track system is very straightforward, and there are two basic techniques for doing so. Both use Peco rail and one involves soldering. The solder method is simply drilling a hole for pins into the sleepers, and soldering the rail to each pin. This does provide a very robust unit, and is less likely to be damaged during track cleaning, but it is not for everyone and lacks the correct rail chairs. A simpler way, and one that uses commercial parts, is using the chair assemblies marketed by Peco and which are designed to work with their track range; most novice modellers will choose these.

Tools required:
• Pin chuck and drills

Materials required:
• Peco track
• Peco Conductor rail chairs, ref. IL – 120
• Peco Code 60 flatbottom conductor rail
• Solvent
• Paint

Work out in advance where the conductor rail would be sited on your track plan. It is probably worth marking where the breaks and joins will be with a felt pen on to the baseboard to avoid mistakes. Then drill a number of holes with a 0.8mm drill at four sleeper intervals at a 1mm distance from the sleeper end. If you are using the standard Code 100 track then you will need the small plastic washer included to bring the pot up to the correct height. It is simply a case of threading the rail on to the required number of chairs, and gently pushing a chair into each pre-drilled hole. The washers can either be fixed over the hole with a drop of solvent, or attached to the 'leg' of the pot beforehand. Either will work.

It is worth pointing out that the pot and chair assembly is small and very fragile, and it is worth threading a couple more than you need, as in most cases you will break a couple during the fitting. When fitted, the pot and chair can be given a tiny drop of solvent to secure them – but use only a tiny drop, as the part is so small that a large wash of liquid could possibly melt it. As always, moderation with any adhesive is good practice.

The conductor rail 'pot' when fitted would have been white. However, the mixture of grease from the shoe, brake dust and general dirt and weathering meant that it did not take long for this to tone down. Even a cursory glance at photos will show that the rail and pot is/was coated in a dark grey sludge. This is, of course, easy to replicate with a fairly generous coat of paint: a mix of black, dark grey and brown applied unevenly will serve admirably. This will contrast nicely against the polished top of the adjacent running rail.

The fitted conductor rail should stand about ½–1mm higher than the running rails. This causes problems with track cleaning, but the cleaning process is likely to damage the third rail if care is not taken. The use of track rubbers is probably best avoided, and instead a soft cloth dipped in solvent or methylated spirit and run along the rail with the finger may prove more reliable – though obviously do this with great care as it is a highly flammable liquid.

RIGHT: **Third rail fitted to Peco Code 100 track.**

BELOW: **The same rail painted and 'weathered' with acrylic paint.**

RAIL POSITION

The position of the conductor rail is critical. It doesn't need to be continuous, but any break or change of side should include a short overlap. Apart from the complication around pointwork, there is a safety element in that where there is likely to be staff and/or pedestrian access, the conductor rail must be moved to the opposite side, or in some cases boarded at the sides. Every location has specific requirements, so it is best to study photos or simply observe from the lineside; however, the basic positioning of the rail away from the passenger platform faces, and in the centre of double track through bridges and tunnels, is standard.

Adding a third rail section to even a simple layout is an easy and visually interesting way once again to pin your model to a Southern area. The only other location in the UK to traditionally use a third rail system is a small area in Merseyside. The next chapter outlines the possible electric units that could be used, and the building of a simple 'track paralleling' (TP) hut power box to add to the flavour.

ABOVE: **South West Trains Class 450 Desiro unit leaves Havant. The photo clearly shows the layout of the third rail around a junction. Note also the amount of staff-generated debris and the cable runs beside the track.**

The third rail switches from the outside of the track to the inside through tunnels; the mouth of this one is behind the camera.

CHAPTER ELEVEN

ELECTRIC UNITS AND A 'TRACK PARALLELING' (TP) HUT

You only have to travel back a few years and the sight of a Southern Region third rail layout in a model magazine was a surprise: they were indeed rare. However, more recently the model manufacturers of ready-to-run equipment have caught up with the movement in which a few short-run kit makers have been participating for quite a while. This is probably because much of the steam-age model market was overdone and saturated, and the manufacturers saw a gap in the market where the modeller could now be sold a pack of motorized carriages. That may seem slightly cynical, but there was such a time gap between the last commercial 4mm-scale electric units produced by Tri-ang in the 1960s and the current breed of high quality models that arrived ten years into the twenty-first century, that it is hard to find a better explanation.

Whatever the reasoning, the positive upshot is that there is now enough available for even the absolute beginner to produce a Southern Region third rail electric layout from ready-to-run items. But where do you start? The development of the system has been covered in the previous chapter, but what were things like post-1948, and what are all those three-letter codes for stock?

THE TELEGRAPHIC CODES

For reasons unknown, the Southern Region clung on to the Southern Railway's telegraphic coding for units long after the rest of the system had gone over to the designations of Class coding for locomotives and units (for example, Class 08 or Class 252). And although the electric units *did* have Class designations (for example, Class 419), the staff and enthusiasts remained wedded to the number and

Preserved BIL unit at Lewes in 1999.

Seaford-bound ex-Silverlink Class 313.

FIRST GENERATION ELECTRIC UNIT CODES (PRE-WAR BUILT)

2 SL: South London. Originally overhead A/C pick up. 1954

2 WIM: Wimbledon line. Originally overhead A/C pick up. 1954

2 NOL: No lavatories. Built from steam-hauled stock. 1959

2 BIL: Two (bi) lavatories. 1971

2 HAL: One lavatory (half lav.). 1971

4 LAV: Four car, one lavatory. 1968

4 COR: Through-corridor unit. 1971. Associated with the Portsmouth line and often called 'Nelsons'

6 PUL: Corridor with Pullman car. 1966

6 PAN: All lavatories and pantry car. 1966

6 CIT: As 6 PUL, but with different trailer car arrangement. 1966

5 BEL (5PUL): 'Brighton Belle'. All Pullman car unit 1973

4 RES: Dining unit with kitchen and dining cars, 1964. Some reformed to 4 PUL, 1966

4 GRI: 4 RES with converted griddle car. 1961–1971

4 BUF: Buffet unit 1971

three-letter references up until the 1980s at least. Once you understand the reasons for the first couple of design names everything drops into place, and for the early units there are two key factors: brakes and toilets. This is not a natural obvious pairing, though this is indeed the reason for most of the first and second generation unit names that the nationalized Southern Region inherited.

The telegraphic codes have little logic, and it is difficult to see why some of them were adopted. Putting a vowel in the centre makes them easy to vocalize, but even this is not consistent, for instance with units such as '4 GRI' (units with a griddle car). The best way to illustrate some of these designations is to list the major players in the form of a table, as seen opposite. The units marked with single dates were introduced under the Southern Railway and indicate the class withdrawal from general service, while those with two dates indicate Southern Region-built units. The short explanations are just brief notes to help the modeller quickly

identify what would be running in a given area and timespan. The long life of many unit combinations meant that in some cases they were greatly altered, while in others they were seen as merely a quick fix to a temporary traffic issue.

What all the above generally have in common is that there is a direct link to either steam-hauled stock or the early electric systems of the LBSCR and the LSWR, and without going into lengthy technical detail, some were either rebuilds of these or at the very least could be regarded as motorized carriages. The middle period stock such as the 2 NOLs even resembled the early twentieth-century pre-group stock, with compartment doors and a multitude of detailed wooden beading.

Once the Bulleid designs started to appear there was a definite shift in design, as had been the case with the steam-hauled carriage stock with a smooth-sided body design and larger rounded corner windows. The 4 SUB units are in many ways the transition units. The early SUB units at

Preserved COR unit in Kent. Known as 'Nelsons', due to their use on the Portsmouth line and their one-eyed appearance caused by the single driver's window and route display.

SUB unit showing the contemporary Bulleid profile: flat face and rounded side windows.

first glance don't look that much different from the NOLs and BILs, but the later batches are dramatically different, with not only the Bulleid-style sides, but a whole new end profile. The previous units were fitted with austere boxy ends with a sloping end roof profile, while the newer units were much more modern, with an almost slab front that emphasized the shape of the sides.

These new suburban units shaped the designs of the post-war units, and sat as a mid-way point before the British Railways Mark I-influenced units appeared. In effect these were the first of the second generation of Southern units and possibly the most stylish that the region had, either before or since. The following table outlines what came next.

SECOND GENERATION SOUTHERN ELECTRIC UNIT CODES (POST-WAR)

Note: Key letters are in **bold**.

4 **SUB**: Four car suburban unit. The initial batches built on a mix of underframes, 1941–51. The last units were withdrawn in 1981. A highly complex class, with two basic body styles, and many changes of arrangement

4 **EPB**: Suburban units with **E**lectro-**P**neumatic **B**rake. The first of the post-war units to shift to buckeye couplers, rather than using standard link-type couplings. 1951–95

2 **EPB**: As above, 1954–95

2 **HAP**: Lavatory and pneumatic brakes (**HA** as in the HAL, **P** as in EPB). 1957–92

4 **CEP**: Through **C**orridor unit. **E**lectro-**P**neumatic brake. Portsmouth and Bognor lines, and throughout Kent. 1956–2005

4 **CIG**: Through **C**orridor Br**ig**hton line stock. 1964–2005

4 **VEP**: **Ve**stibule, **P**neumatic brake units with high density seating and doors. 1967–2005

3 **COP**: **C**oastway **O**pen **P**lan. Downgraded BIG/CIG units; some were later enlarged to 4 COP (or 3 CIG with the 3 COP number range). These were the final representatives of the second generation, and mainly used on the Sussex/Hampshire coasts. 1997–2005

HAP unit enters Newhaven Harbour station in 1979 with CIG unit in the distance standing in the now defunct, but not officially closed, Newhaven Marine station.

The above tables are purely a simple overview of basic electric multiple-unit classes. Within this there are many detail differences. For instance, some HAPs were downgraded to second class for a while and reclassified SAP, only to have the first class reinstated, and then later taken away again. You will notice that many of these unit classes had longer working lives than many of the steam locomotive classes that had preceded them, some with a fifty-year span. This meant that most were refitted and overhauled many times over, creating a multitude of detail differences.

It is recommended that the student and modeller of the third-rail unit obtains one or two of the excellent guides to these classes, several of which were published at the time of the final withdrawal of these 'slam-door' units in 2004/5. The reason for this wholesale removal of units was legislation in the last decade of the twentieth century following crash investigations that found that the wooden-bodied designs of these second-generation units were no longer fit for purpose on a mainline railway service and that they should be removed as soon as possible; the wood frames had more in common with nineteenth-century carriage building than the modern metal frames found elsewhere in Europe.

Due to several factors this ditching of the second generation did not happen as quickly as was envisaged, and many hung on until 2005, some eleven years after the official end of British Rail, although there were instances of 3 COP/3 CIGs being run to Lymington beyond that date.

3 COP at Bishopstone in 2003: these were the final slam-door units on this route before the ban on wooden-framed stock came into force.

New, sliding-door metal-bodied units started to appear on the Southern Region as early as 1979 with the brief stay of the Class 508, but it was not until the beginning of privatization that the death knell sounded for the slam-door stock.

BEFORE AND AFTER PRIVATIZATION

MODELLING THE EARLIER UNITS

The modeller wishing to represent some of the earlier units is currently well served, and the situation looks to improve all the time. There are ready-to-run models of HALs, HAPs, CEPs and BILs in 4mm scale, with probably more due. Bearing in mind that most lines similar to our layout idea above would have seen only a couple of unit classes at any one time, this small but growing stud of models would be plenty to get you going. Also it would be possible to fill in any gaps by using kits from the smaller manufacturers such as DC Kits,

who produce a large range of Southern Region unit models.

POST-SOUTHERN REGION AND THE QUIET PRIVATIZATION

From 1986 a large portion of the British Rail Southern Region came under a branding exercise known as Network SouthEast, which operated independently of BR. This paralleled several other branding exercises around the country, such as the 'sectorization' of the freight operations. This was, of course, the precursor to privatization, and was a thinly veiled operation to make certain areas of the rail network look attractive in small increments, which could then be given over to private operating companies.

As far as the modeller is concerned, Network Southeast was a re-livery of rolling stock, with most of the units and locomotives, even including some Class 50s, being painted in red, blue and white stripes (initially referred to by some enthusiasts as 'toothpaste livery', for obvious reasons). Attractive though this was, especially after years of

A CEP unit rolls into Ashford. First designed for the London–Portsmouth services, the CEPs became synonymous with Kent line traffic.

A CIG crosses Glynde Reach in 1991 wearing Network SouthEast livery.

blue and grey on everything, the carriage washing plants did not treat the livery kindly, and the red soon scrubbed off or turned pink under sunlight. This pre-privatization period has, however, lately become a nostalgic era to represent, and there are models being brought out in special packs with this paintwork design. So if this post-1986, pre-1994 period appeals to you, there is actually quite a lot available, and also plenty of prototype information to hand.

POST-PRIVATIZATION

Strictly speaking, our subject matter of British Railways Southern Region ceased to exist in 1994 when the system was split up and offered to franchises that actually operated the trains themselves, and a separate company, Railtrack, which was responsible for the care and maintenance of the track and signalling. The twenty-plus years since have been rocky at times in what was a political move to reverse the nationalization process of the 1940s. There have, however, been great improvements in the whole system, which can be directly

linked to this change, which probably would never have happened under British Rail, as it had become renamed some thirty years earlier. Conversely, at the time of writing, there are calls from some quarters to reverse this once again and re-nationalize the rail network. So there may be a return to blue and grey rolling stock yet.

THE NEW DAWN OF PRIVATE COMPANIES

Although it is out of the given timescale of this book, it is worth looking briefly at the electric units post-privatization. Two companies initially took control: Stagecoach in the west of the region and Connex in the east. Later Govia, under the brand 'Southern', took over the central section, and the eastern section returned into government control until 2006 when it, too, was taken over by Govia. Initially the rolling stock was given new liveries, but not much else changed; the second-generation CEPs and CIGs still clung on amongst the newer sliding-door classes.

CIG 1801 leads a pair of sets in livery transition, the first in Network SouthEast 'toothpaste', the second in Connex yellow and white.

It wasn't until 1999 that the Electrostar Class 377 and Desiro Class 450 and Class 444 were introduced, and started to dent the slam-door unit numbers. In 2005 the safety regulations bit hard, and there were enough available to wipe the slam doors away for good. At the time of writing this is still essentially the state of play. A few new units have come and gone, as has the unique Gatwick Express consist of Mark 2 carriage stock, with a Class 73 electro-diesel at one end and an MLV (motor luggage van) at the other – now replaced by Class 460.

It is interesting to realize that the post-nationalization period – 1994 to the current time – is now as long as what some would consider to be the previous classic period of the Southern Railway, and that we have in some ways just returned to the days before 1923, with many separate railway companies covering the United Kingdom, a situation that the 1920s government was keen to abolish. History continually repeats itself.

Despite this long, modern privatized period, modellers are much more likely to look back to a previous mainly steam-driven age. The reasons for this are complex: perhaps it is a desire to represent what may be considered to be a gentler, more serene period of history, maybe a period in

Gatwick Express unit accelerates away from Gatwick Airport with the MLV driving end leading and a Class 73 electro-diesel pushing from the rear.

EPBs stand at Eastbourne in the sunshine. Although still in 'rail blue and grey', they are badged with NSE flashes on the ends and cabs.

which the modeller grew up, albeit one that was many times more polluting and lacking in health and safety; or perhaps it is the perceived lack of operation that running model multiple units would give. Whatever it is, this earlier time is by far the more popular amongst enthusiasts and modellers alike.

A SOUTHERN REGION TRACK PARALLELING (TP) HUT

Modelling (or just suggesting) third rail running is fairly straightforward: a simple length of rail added to plain track as described in the previous chapter, and a short two-car unit would be all that you would need – but where does all the power come from? In simple terms, power is taken from the grid and reset for the third rail via a set of transformer/substations. These are still visible at many station sites, although many are a shadow of their former selves, both internally and externally: the march of technology has reduced the size of the equipment

required, and in some cases the buildings have been bypassed altogether. The size of the buildings varies from site to site, but because in the main they are close to platform areas, they are easy to observe.

For the 4mm-scale modeller there is a useful resin model of one of these substation buildings available from Bachmann. It is slightly under scale, but this is hardly noticeable and most modellers will accept the size. However, that is not the whole story. The problem with the relatively low voltage

TIP: USE GOOGLE EARTH TO SURVEY RAIL LINES

Use an internet site such as Google Earth to visually survey rail lines and find out where the substations and track paralleling (TP) huts are located.

ABOVE: **Substation near Norman's Bay. Note the position of the far third rail.**

Offham track paralleling hut, disappearing under nettle growth. This TP has a filled window, high vents and a security camera.

used on the Southern Region was that over a length of line there was a fall in power strength. This was overcome by what was called 'double-end feeding'. As it suggests, there was another set of power feeds at the other end of the section from the substation, and this required a small building to house the equipment, known as a 'track paralleling' hut – or 'TP' hut for short.

As can be seen from the photographs, the TP hut is a standard Southern Region design, essentially plain with very little in the way of non-essential fittings and no decoration. The huts vary very slightly from site to site, and in recent years many have had any windows blocked off. This is mainly due to the upsurge in break-ins to steal copper wiring for resale as scrap metal. Needless to say security is high. This, combined with the decision in recent times not to cut back lineside vegetation, makes the TP huts difficult to research and photograph. It does, of course, go without saying that climbing through all the nettles to do this is at best trespassing and at worst could result in fatal electrocution. It is therefore strongly recommended that you stay behind the fence.

By their very nature these buildings were generally sited away from the main station, on open sections of line, but they will provide the modeller with another visual clue to third rail use and place; they are also usefully space saving on a layout, as compared to the full substation. Furthermore, because no commercial model is available at the time of writing, this is another occasion where a little scratch building can take place – and they are simple enough to make from more or less scrap material. If you have built some of the earlier projects, then much of what is needed will already be to hand.

PROJECT SEVENTEEN: SOUTHERN REGION TRACK PARALLELING (TP) HUT

Tools required:
- Knife
- Solvent
- Sanding stick and files
- Sanding block

Ashcombe track paralleling hut: lower vents and a grill-backed window, and a phone cabinet just out of view.

Materials required:
- 60-thou plastic sheet, or reversed Wills sheet
- Wills window and door
- 20-thou sheet (scrap)
- 30-thou sheet (scrap)
- Tissue paper
- 20 × 10-thou plastic strip
- Glazing

THE WALLS

The hut itself (though hut is a misleading description) is a one-and-a-half storey building built from block with a rendered finish. The roof is slightly sloping and is covered with a lead or roofing felt material. There is usually only a single window and door, but there are small sloping vents on all the walls.

Four walls need to be cut from 60-thou plastic sheet to the following sizes: front, 60mm wide by 59mm high; back, 60mm wide by 55mm high; and the two ends 46mm wide by 59mm, falling to 55mm. Mark the sizes in pencil on the sheet and add a 'T' to indicate the top. Mitre all joining edges to just under 45 degrees, as with the Wills sheet used in earlier building projects.

Mark a window opening on the back wall 19mm wide by 12mm deep, set 28mm from the foot of the wall, and drill out and file to shape as usual.

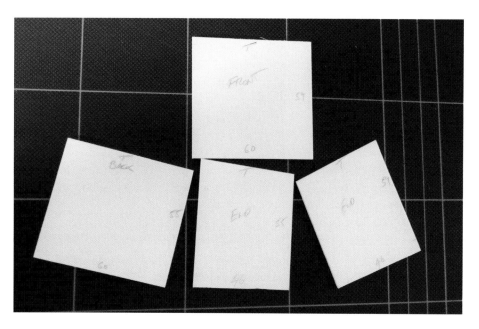

Track paralleling hut walls from 60-thou plastic. All measurements are marked in pencil to aid construction.

On one end wall mark a doorway 27mm high by 14mm wide, and set in from the back by 4mm. Add the window and door from the Wills building pack (if you have built the earlier station building these should be spares from the kit), and edge the door with 20- × 10-thou strip to represent the frame.

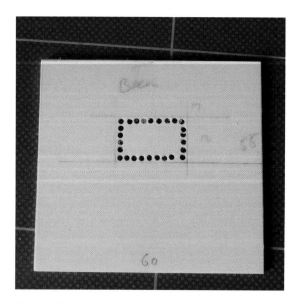

Rear wall with the window in the process of being drilled out.

DETAILS

Cut a piece of 20-thou plastic sheet to a size of 6.5mm square. Then cut a similar piece of 30- or 40-thou 5.5mm square. The second piece should be sanded on one face to a wedge shape to represent the slope of the wall ventilator. When this shape has been achieved, add the wedge to the thin sheet. This is very possibly a scrap plastic process, using offcuts from previous projects. Card could be substituted instead. Repeat this four times, and add the first to the back wall 5mm down from the top and 8mm from the edge. Add the end vent level with this, also 8mm from the edge.

Tiny sloping vents from 20- and 30-thou plastic sheet.

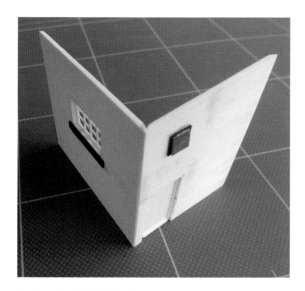

First pair of Wills fixed square.

Join the end and back wall as shown, check that the join is square, and repeat with the front and other end wall after adding the vents, then joining the two pairs. At least two internal corners should be reinforced with a triangular fillet from scrap plastic sheet.

A smaller ventilator cover plate can be made up from a 4mm square piece of 20-thou sheet and four lengths of 20 × 10-thou strip. This can be added to the back wall 9mm down from the top and 11mm in from the edge.

Small vent made from 20-thou sheet and strip plastic.

THE ROOF

A roof piece can be cut from 60-thou sheet, or as here, a piece of Wills sheet of the same thickness, but which needs to be sanded to remove any mould lines. The size here is 64 × 50mm, giving a 2mm overhang all the way round. To represent the roof texture a single sheet of tissue paper should be stuck to the top using a wash of solvent. This will probably cause the plastic to bow in at least one plane, so add a bracing piece as shown to keep the sheet flat.

Roof made from building sheet, covered with tissue paper and braced to stop curling.

Roof fitted, showing the tissue 'texture' effect.

Tidy up the edges of the tissue paper and stick down firmly, then add the roof to the constructed walls. Finally add a window ledge from a strip of 30-thou plastic 25 × 3mm in size.

PAINTING

Paint the structure to suit: the walls are usually plain rendered cement colour, so the usual mix of

Glazing should be sanded in two directions to represent grills and the general filth inside.

Humbrol 64 (light grey) and 63 (sand) will work well. The woodwork can be any suitable colour, but as usual, green predominates. The roof should be a lead grey. When the painting is complete, add a piece of glazing behind the window unit. Here the plastic has been 'scratched' in two directions with a sanding stick to simulate mesh glass. Without fail these windows (if not bricked up) are usually filthy, and you just need to show that the glass is there and do not necessarily need to make it transparent.

OTHER DETAILS

Depending on your model period, the buildings can vary in detail. Some have gutters and downpipes, others not. Middle period structures have a small phone cabinet by the door, and more modern huts have CCTV cameras mounted high on the walls. In this project a phone cabinet has been added made from a length of square sprue from the concrete platelayers' hut – nothing is wasted!

Make sure your hut is bedded into the layout with plenty of undergrowth around it, and remember to break the third rail in front of it and add the feed wiring. It's also possible to have a barrow crossing in the front if the staff access is on the other side of the track.

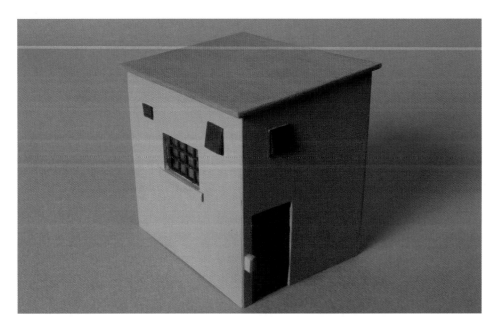

Completed TP hut.

CHAPTER TWELVE

DIESEL UNITS

THE PROBLEM AND THE SOLUTION

If the Southern steam engine was the glamorous older sister and the electric the super-efficient younger brother, then the diesel was the Southern Region's difficult middle child. The Southern Region had several problems to solve, the biggest being how to modernize with as small a budget as possible. As discussed in the previous two chapters, the main thrust was to electrify the main routes and gradually withdraw the steam-hauled stock.

The problem therefore was twofold: first, the possibility of electrifying the entire system was unlikely, at least in the near future; and second, it was obvious by the mid-1950s that steam would be removed from the system, leaving all the non-electrified lines without independent power. In many cases lines were proving to be uneconomic to operate, whether electrified or not. The Southern's public persona was one of a forward-thinking system with efficient electric trains, but any journey of reasonable length on the system usually meant that a part of your trip was behind a steam locomotive built when Queen Victoria was still on the throne.

The Southern's plan (as with all British Railways' regions) was to develop a couple of diesel designs to replace the steam-hauled stock. Logically the region would have followed the example of the other parts of the British Isles and introduced a series of railcars that drew heavily on contemporary bus technology, with large open units with big windows and underfloor engines. The Southern Region, however, typically ran counter to the whole of the rest of the British Isles and built a set of diesel units that aesthetically echoed the contemporary electric units; and instead of using under-floor power, they elected to mount the diesel engine above the floor next to the passenger compartment, thereby taking up 25

per cent of the available seating space in one carriage.

These units, unlike the bus-derived units, were diesel generators powering the standard electric traction units, and not direct diesel engine to gearbox as the bus units. Hence the Southern Region's units are not DMU (diesel multiple unit) but DEMU (diesel electric multiple unit).

THE WIDTH PROBLEM AGAIN

Part of the reason behind the choice of this type of machine was that the standard shape British DMU was unsuitable, because the width of the gauge was again a problem. The tunnels on the eastern side of the Southern Region could only be through-operated by steam stock, which had essentially been doing the work for decades, so the Southern Region had first to solve this problem before steam traction could be abandoned. Interlaced track was considered briefly, while singling the line was considered unsafe due to the heavy frequency of the traffic. It was decided that the only way forwards was to follow the lead of the previous companies and create a stud of dedicated narrow-width trains to work this part of the system.

THE 'HASTINGS' UNITS

The result was a plan for twenty-three six-car units of three types: 6S (shorter cars), 6L (longer cars), and 6B, which was a long car unit including a buffet car. These usually ran as twelve-car sets, which could be split mid-journey depending on traffic flows. The units had a long life and ran until the mid-1980s, when it was decided that safety technology had improved sufficiently to allow the offending sections of line to be reduced to single-line working and subsequently electrified. The introduction of what were referred to as the 'Hastings' units in 1957–8 was really a game changer on the Southern

ABOVE: **Hastings unit running in green livery in the early 1980s.**

Hastings unit in standard blue-grey stands at Ashford.

Region, and although the outward design was seen as somewhat retrograde at the time, the success of the Hastings units opened up the way for the abolition of steam all over the Southern Region.

The addenda to the Hastings story are the 3R units. By the mid-1960s there was a requirement for a small unit to run the inter-regional service from Redhill to Reading. A reduction of service to the east allowed the power cars from the Hastings units to be coupled to one of the Hastings trailer cars, and a driving end from a redundant 2 EPB. This created an odd formation, with the combination of the flat slab-sided Hastings cars and the more rotund profile of the Bulleid EPB presenting a fat-to-thin appearance, giving rise to the name 'Tadpole' units. Once again the Tadpoles proved highly successful on the route from 1965, and were only displaced in 1979 by redundant Western Region Class 119 DMUs.

At the time of writing there are no Hastings units available ready to run in any scale. However, there have been several kits available over the years, notably and most recently in 4mm from DC Kits, which are fairly straightforward ABS plastic designs, powered by a separately available motorized power bogie. It is, however, only a matter of time before a Hastings unit appears on the manufacturers' listings in 4mm scale 'out of the box'.

THE STEAM-RUN BRANCHES

British Railways' 1955 modernization plan was in some ways very late arriving as compared to other countries. The rise of the private car and road freight haulage after World War II had spurred the Transport Commission into looking at a major streamlining of rail use. Some of this was political pressure, and several historical reports have underlined how loudly the lobby for road expansion was shouting during the period 1950 to 1970. Railways were seen as the past, and the internal combustion engine as cleaner and more flexible in usage.

It is easy to include the Southern Railway's and Southern Region's push for electric traction in with this, which of course is wrong, as the electrification plans had originated from a point before World War

I, and when the country was in a different frame of mind altogether. This was not nationally about purely electric traction in the south, it was about reducing the rail network to a bare minimum, and pushing as much traffic on to the roads as possible, and for any remaining non-electric lines to be diesel operated.

We understand now that diesel emissions are far from clean, but it is hard for the modern enthusiast to comprehend just how filthy a concentration of steam locomotives could be. The preserved lines of today can only hint at this. In the main they are in rural settings and are only running one or two locomotives at any one time, and the dirty business of tons of dusty coal and piles of waste ash are kept well away from public areas. Prior to the 1950s, travelling by train in the British Isles was a physically dirty pastime, with stations and carriage seats coated in a layer of fine ash and smuts. In operating terms, running a diesel fleet for suburban and secondary routes was, compared to steam, much lower in maintenance and didn't require a lot of man hours and preparing the locomotive: it just involved the turn of a key. Super-clean diesel was the future.

REPLACING STEAM

The previous chapter outlined the three growth spurts of the electric system, but by the mid-1950s this had still covered only a portion of the Southern Region; many of the secondary lines were still operated by pre-group locomotives, which in many cases were soon to be replaced by the British Rail 'standard' tank classes – though these were only a stopgap. What was needed was a clean diesel train similar to the electric units that had proved so popular. Hampshire was the first area of the region to demand these on the routes around Southampton, Salisbury and Winchester.

The machine devised for this job was a short two-car unit that would be diesel powered. But once again for some reason the Southern Region discounted the bus-inspired units that were being introduced all over the rest of the British Isles and, following in the footsteps of the Hastings units, designed an above-floor mounted diesel-engine

LEFT: **2H Hampshire DEMU 'Thumper' newly arrived at Uckfield in 1999.**

BELOW: **3D Oxted unit stands at Eastbourne. Note the rounded roof profile as compared to the Hampshire units, as well as the recessed MU connectors. The triangle denotes the motor driving end.**

machine with 600hp of output feeding electric traction motors. Unlike the Hastings units, these were built to full-width body style and were outwardly similar to the later EPB electric units.

Why this happened is not immediately obvious, as this time there was no need to design a unit specifically for a Southern route – one of the DMU classes used further north would have worked just as well. Needless to say the two-car units (designated 2H, later Class 205) began work in the area in 1957. They were successful, but low capacity, and were strengthened to three-car units with the addition of a second-class trailer (designated 3H).

Popular though they were, the 2H/3H units did not completely supersede the steam-hauled trains, and these were still running at peak times until the middle of the 1960s. The Southern Region was content that the units were viable, and another batch was built to operate the non-electric, non-width restricted routes around Hastings, and later still saw use on the lines from Oxted, Tunbridge Wells and Lewes.

As many of their original routes were cut back, the 2H/3Hs were moved further out and covered even electrified route workings, but with boundary changes their original area was (logically) worked by Western Region DMUs from 1973.

A STREAMLINED THUMPER

Following the success of the 3H units on the Sussex coast, a new batch of diesels was ordered to work the north–south routes around Oxted and East Grinstead, and entered service in 1962. These were designated 3D (Oxted, later Class 207), and

The replacement from 2004. Class 171 DMU waits at Uckfield in 2005. Note also the upgraded passenger facilities since the earlier photos.

differed from the Hastings and Hampshire machines by having a more rounded profile, and inset boxes to house the multiple unit connection piping. The power output was also reduced to 500hp. Essentially these two classes were interchangeable in working, and although the 3Ds were a rarity in Hampshire, both the 3Hs and the 3Ds worked side by side in Sussex and West Kent.

Although the wide-gauge thumper units were greatly reduced in numbers as more of their home ground was electrified in the 1980s, a stalwart band of them was still working into the post-privatization years in Connex livery. They were not withdrawn until the 'slam-door' purges of 2004, and were mostly replaced by new under-floor motored Class 171 two-car diesel units.

MODELLING

The modeller of the non-electric Southern Region was badly served until recent times. The diesel units are a boon, as not only can they be theoretically run anywhere, but they allow the Southern modeller to use a 'pure breed' Southern Region unit (again defining the place) without the need for laying metres of third rail on the layout. There have been kits available, again in recent times from DC Kits, but from 2015 a joint production from Kernow Models and Bachmann turned out a stunning ready-to-run 2H/205 in a variety of liveries from original British Railways green to the red, white and blue of Network SouthEast. While these models are hardly in the pocket-money price bracket, the quality is

Uckfield signal box and platform end. The line continued across the road to the original station, but was cut back during the 1980s.

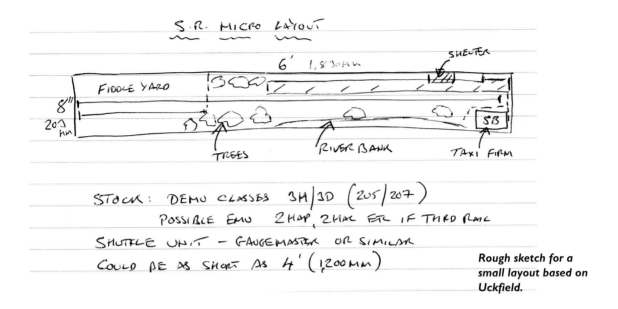

Rough sketch for a small layout based on Uckfield.

extremely high and they are a 'must buy' item for the non-electric unit modeller.

As these 3H and 3D units were essentially direct replacements for the steam branch and secondary services, it is perfectly possible to take any of the rough plans included (or any branch-line track plan) and project a thumper unit into the picture. Taking the scenario of the branch terminus operated by a Terrier tank engine and a basic set of stock, it would be easily possible to substitute some trains with a diesel unit, or indeed run all the passenger services thus. Tail traffic (adding a van to the rear of a diesel unit) is not documented, but as other regions did use this method of transporting a small quantity of parcels, there seems no reason why this consist of train could not be accommodated to add interest to the operating.

For a really basic layout for the modeller with absolutely no space, something based on the twenty-first-century Uckfield station would be an excuse for a tiny layout for a bookshelf, with just a thumper in Network SouthEast or Connex livery running in and out, maybe powered by an electronic shuttle unit. Albeit pointless in both senses of the phrase, it is an excuse for some limited space modelling that is Southern Region inspired. The next couple of photographs show how this could be done.

A PLAN FOR THE MODELLER WITH LITTLE SPACE

The micro-layout is very much in vogue these days, most of them based around either narrow-gauge lines or they are shunting puzzles. This plan isn't exactly a micro, but for the prototype rolling stock involved it is very small. The modeller in mind for this plan is either the stressed executive with no time who wants something to sit on a shelf in the office, or the complete novice who wants to attempt something Southern Region without having to spend too much for stock or building materials. The prototype inspiration for the plan is quite logical: the Oxted to Lewes line was truncated in 1969, not as part of railway cutbacks, but to allow a road scheme to progress. The new route terminated at Uckfield station, and all track to the south was lifted.

The issue that for many years caused problems was that the station was on the wrong side of Uckfield High Street. This meant that all trains required the road gates to be closed to access the station, even though the train travelled only a few yards further on before it stopped. By the 1980s the pressure from the town was so great that the station was moved to the north of the road, and the road crossing closed. As the line was already run with DEMU thumper units, only a single platform with

3H Hampshire unit leaves Uckfield platform and heads towards Oxted.

rudimentary shelter and facilities was provided: the ultimate in a stripped-down railway station.

MODELLING UCKFIELD

As the platform is only 1 metre long in 4mm OO scale, and the two-car units are only a little over half a metre long, it would be quite possible to build the station to scale complete with a fiddle (storage) yard for somewhere to run the unit from in less than 2 metres. This length could even be reduced slightly and still retain the prototype feel. The site is edged on the west side by the River Uck (in fact the platform partially bridges it) and to the east side by a car dealership, which could be represented in low relief on the backscene. The original LBSCR signalbox is a listed building, and has been restored and occupied by a local taxi company. This forms a useful visual stop and frame to the layout. The other end of the site is tree-lined, and these trees could form the visual break before the line disappears into the storage yard.

The down side is that the operation is minimal. It could be operated by an electronic shuttle unit – but a high operation layout is not the point. The novice modeller is often put off by having a large expanse of baseboard to cover with track and scenery, and this rough idea allows him or her to try a few ideas and build up confidence before tackling something much larger. If electric units are desired, then it is only a small step to add a third rail to the single line. Doing this means that both electric and diesel units could be used. The plan could also be employed by the more experienced modeller who wants to try a new, or several new, scenic techniques without risking a whole large layout project.

TIP: LOOK AT LESS OBVIOUS STATION PLANS

Don't be afraid to look at less obvious station plans, whether simple like this Uckfield one, or more complex. Sites such as parcels depots and passing loops make just as good models as the traditional terminus station shape.

Blue-grey CIG units at Lewes in 1985.

CHAPTER THIRTEEN

CONCLUSIONS

Modelling the Southern Region is a fascinating and absorbing subject for a model railway, and the surface has only been scratched here. Any book can only deal with certain aspects of a subject, and the thrust of this volume was to look at what may be possible in order to nudge the modeller (especially the novice) into thinking slightly 'outside the box'. The model trade has of late provided an enormous amount of help to achieve the perfect layout, particularly in the popular scale of 4mm/OO. However, what I have tried to show throughout the book is that while most of these products are of top quality,

they can sometimes lead the modeller down a slightly un-prototypical road.

This is not wrong or deliberately misleading – after all, tradespeople are in the business of selling as many units as possible – but sometimes the labelling can be slightly confusing; it is not necessarily inaccurate, but sometimes the newer (and even more experienced) modeller is led to believe that a particular item may be the historically correct one. This may be the case, but where the modeller may take all this packet-header card information as historical fact, in many cases a particular item may not

Uckfield-bound Hampshire unit pauses at Eridge in 2004. Single-line working applied at this time.

A suburban station in a cutting would present a very different model scenario; the over-track station building here at Tadworth gives a perfect scenic break into the fiddle yard.

in fact have found widespread use until long after the implied date, if at all. Or in the case of some rolling stock, it may have been long time expired within the early years of the Southern Region, and therefore untypical past the mid-1950s modernization plan.

RESEARCH

Only a few years ago it was necessary to purchase a large number of photo album-type books to gather information. Now, however, the internet can provide the same sort of information in seconds. The warning here is that publishers of books are more careful in dating photos, where the internet

is rather more casual in interpretation. The best of the current publications for this is the huge range published by Middleton Press, which has covered most, if not all the lines in the Southern Region area almost station by station. This is a great boon for the modeller, as it is possible to pick a couple of typical lines that are close to the prospective layout's style, and accurately pinpoint what would have run and what signalling hardware and lineside structures would have been typical at any point in the historical time spread.

As I have pointed out repeatedly throughout this book, it is this typicality that is of paramount importance in getting a model to 'feel' right, and the one thing that will lift any layout to being a true model railway and not an off-the-shelf trainset. Magazines often feature layouts that, while beautifully executed, have obviously not taken this into account: for instance they might give the modelled date as 1965, yet have strings of attractively coloured 'private owner' wagons in pristine original paint styles. The reality, of course, would be that if the wagons had survived that long, they would be in terrible condition, painted in standard British Railways unfitted grey, or been heavily patched with unpainted replacement planks. The modeller has been drawn in by the name of a local coal merchant or home yard, but has done no research to see if they would have actually run during the given period. The result is a beautiful layout but with no illusion of reality – it is a model collection.

This is not to imply any fine-scale snobbery, only that if you are going to buy/build a wagon and spend, say, £10 on it, then you may as well invest your time and money into a wagon that fits the period you are modelling.

EXHIBITING

In the early chapters I mentioned that during the planning process it should be considered whether the layout being built will be exhibited. This isn't always something that can be added at a later date. A layout that has been built for a specific home situation may be tricky to operate in public, and may also be impossible to move using the family car. While this last point doesn't preclude taking a layout to a show, the extra cost involved in van hire

Perfect Southern Region stock dating on Crawley MRS's Gauge O-scale Harlyn Road.

Excellent Southern Region electric stock such as this 4COR is a feature of Paul Hopkins' Retford in 3mm scale.

and so on may make the outing more difficult on cost grounds. Exhibition managers usually operate on a tight budget, and the allowance for van hire is usually only factored in for large club-type layouts.

The other consideration is that of entertainment value, not only for the exhibition visitor, but also for you the operator. For instance the layout idea in the foregoing chapter would not be at all suitable: as an experimental test or on an office shelf environment it may work very well, but for a fourteen-hour, two-day exhibition, as the operator you would be unacceptably bored within an hour. Building exhibition layouts is very much a 'horses for courses' planning exercise.

Specifically a Southern Region layout that is to be exhibited should have a few basic ideals factored in:

first, on a visual level it should be instantly recognizable as part of the region before any trains appear. Second, those trains should represent as accurately a possible the kind of stock that ran in the given area and time span; and third, it should be entertaining to view and operate for the reasons given above. Failure to commit to the first two points is acceptable on a home layout when you have no one to please but yourself, but once you make that jump into the public sphere there will be countless knowledgeable people who will take great pains to inform you that you have got it all wrong. It is expected that you will have done at least some basic research and be able to explain any oddities.

Don't let this put you off, however, as there will be just as many people willing to offer advice and more information, especially if you have based your layout on a prototype scene. This holds especially true if you exhibit within the Southern Region area, as it won't take long for retired railway staff to come forwards and offer detailed explanations of working practices – and they will often praise the fact that you have come very close to the actuality.

The third point covers entertaining. While a small percentage of the visitors at a model railway exhibition will be highly knowledgeable, the larger percentage will be casual visitors with only a basic interest, and very little idea of how a railway works. Although the exhibitor is not specifically there to educate, it does help if the physical moves made by the train on the layout are frequent in order to hold the viewer's attention, but the layout should also

replicate as closely as possible the correct stock and signal movements. This adds a certain authenticity to the occasion, and helps to dispel the attitude held by some people that this is grown men playing trains.

Having a timetable or sequence in either paper or digital form displayed in easy view also helps to explain what is happening on scene. If you are modelling the Southern Region steam period, then it is worth taking into consideration that two generations have grown up since the end of steam, and anyone under fifty years old will not remember it on British Railways. As a proportion of the exhibition audience is likely to be young families, giving as much information on and around the layout is helpful and may draw more young people into the hobby.

Brighton-built 80104 arrives at Swanage in 2015.

Southern Region modelling is really no different from working on any other part of the British Isles rail system. All have a make-up of pre-grouping companies and their own particular brand of traffic flow. The northern and midland regions had greater coal and mineral traffic, as did the South Wales valleys, but the further you move from the capital, so the intensity of the passenger traffic fades a little. The Southern was unique in that it served – and still serves – a commuter and holiday passenger trade like no other region, and although it was not the first to embrace the new technology of the internal combustion engine on passenger routes, it does, with a mix of steam, diesel and electric, give the modeller by far the widest choices in motive power.

Besides which, as everyone knows, the sun always shines on the Southern.

The Southern today. Here, Class 377 bound for Brighton pulls into Bedhampton in Hampshire. Almost all traces of the building company the LBSCR, and the Southern Region, have disappeared now. Only the footbridge from where the photograph is taken gives any reference to past days.

INDEX

RELATED TITLES FROM CROWOOD

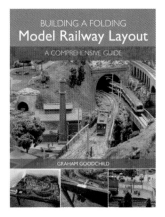

Building a Folding Model Railway Layout

GRAHAM GOODCHILD

ISBN 978 1 78500 199 4

192pp, 315 illustrations

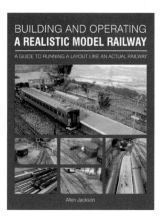

Building and Operating a Realistic Model Railway

ALLEN JACKSON

ISBN 978 1 78500 169 7

176pp, 260 illustrations

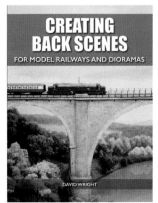

Creating Back Scenes for Model Railways and Dioramas

DAVID WRIGHT

ISBN 978 1 78500 280 9

192pp, 320 illustrations

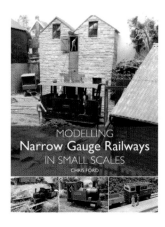

Modelling Narrow Gauge Railways in Small Scales

CHRIS FORD

ISBN 978 1 84797 935 3

176pp, 220 illustrations

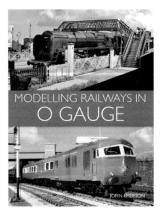

Modelling Railways in O Gauge

JOHN EMERSON

ISBN 978 1 78500 254 0

192pp, 260 illustrations

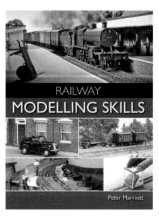

Railway Modelling Skills

PETER MARRIOTT

ISBN 978 1 84797 955 1

224pp, 400 illustrations

In case of difficulty ordering, please contact the Sales Office:

The Crowood Press, Ramsbury, Wiltshire SN8 2HR UK

Tel: 44 (0) 1672 520320   enquiries@crowood.com   www.crowood.com